THE
HANDBOOK
OF
DEVELOPMENTAL DISABILITIES AND REHABILITATION

DR NEERJA PANDEY

PARTRIDGE

To order additional copies of this book, contact
Partridge India
000 800 919 0634 (Call Free)
+91 000 80091 90634 (Outside India)
orders.india@partridgepublishing.com

www.partridgepublishing.com/india

CONTENTS

FOREWORD

The **"Handbook of Developmental Disabilities and Rehabilitation"** By Dr. Neerja Pandey is an exciting textbook representing clear, engaging and thought-provoking study of disability.

In recent years, our understanding of disability has changed dramatically. This Handbook charts both traditional and contemporary approaches and focuses on the Bio-Psycho-Social Model of Disability.

The book highlights the global nature of disability, the seminal feature being case studies and insights into rehabilitation. Comprehensive in scope, it examines the issues involved in socio – political, social justice and Rights approach to disability. The Handbook makes a significant contribution in developing a new perspective of disability.

The Handbook is readable, scholarly and thoughtful which should be set as a textbook on disability studies courses. It has a clear and coherent format with emphasis on interdisciplinary framework of disability. The Handbook will be indispensable for students seeking to understand disability in a holistic perspective. The book should be on academic agenda and is a must for all self-respecting scholars in the field of disability.

Dr. Neerja Pandey has written a ground breaking book that injects new energy into Disability studies. She made a lucid practical and theoretical connection that is critical and transformative. She has accomplished what many in disability studies in Education and Psychology have hoped for a textbook of high calibre covering broad overview of disability. This handbook is undoubtedly a very welcome addition to the resources of disability studies in India.

Dr. Saroj Arya
President, Association of Rehabilitation Psychologists India (ARPI).

Dr Saroj Arya is:

- Former Associate Professor & Head of the 'Department of Rehabilitation Psychology', NIEPID, Secunderabad
- Currently, Professor in Clinical Psychology, Sweekar Academy of Rehabilitation sciences, Secunderabad.
- Research experience of carrying out multi-centric research studies in the field of Psychology, Nutrition, Mental Health and Disability Rehabilitation.
- Developed Indian Tools for Child Development Assessment and Autism & Manuals for Cognitive enhancement in early childhood.
- Recipient of British Technical Cooperation Training Award under Colombo Plan, University of London
- Recipient of Asha Nigam Award for significant work in Child and Adolescent Mental Health by IACP for the year 2006. Kang Award for significant work in Clinical Psychology by IACP for the year 2007.
- Reeta Peshawaria Fellowship Award for significant work in Child Development & Disability Rehabilitation 2017.
- Fellow Member of Indian Association of Clinical Psychologists.
- Member of International Council of Psychologists,
- Member of Nutrition Society of India and Rehabilitation Council of India.

PREFACE

The intention behind writing the book titled **'The Handbook of Developmental Disabilities and Rehabilitation'** is to provide subject matter on disabilities to college and university students studying Psychology. The author has written the chapters based on her own experiences of being school teacher for five years, being a school-counsellor for five years, studying rehabilitation psychology in MPhil, teaching the subject in Undergraduate as well as Postgraduate courses and finally, realizing the dearth of easy-to-understand and readily available reading material for Indian students. She also has included the notes she had prepared while studying in MPhil and that is why source of information on various topics is missing.

This book is written as a textbook that encompasses all the essential information regarding developmental disabilities including proformas that can be used in clinical practice. This book hence takes a further step from the general theoretical knowledge regarding developmental disabilities and allows glimpses into the formal clinical practice through case studies.

It is kind of easy reckoner and a wholesome book for students and it addresses the related issues and bridges them to rehabilitation by including Individualized Education Plan (preparation, management and plan of action) as well as the Behaviour Modification Techniques (intervention) in it.

She has tried not only to explain the subject matter in simple language but also to maintain the depth and detail of the topics covered. The topics covered in the book are the concept of developmental disabilities, causes of disabilities and case studies.

1. Disabilities – An Introduction. The chapter covers the introduction on developmental disabilities by explaining

other related terms. It is important to study the role of Indian Government in the field of disabilities hence different Acts in developmental disabilities is mentioned by making sure to highlight the certain privileges provided to people with disabilities.

2. Causes of Disabilities and their Prevention. The topics covered in this chapter are prevention at three levels, factors that may negatively affect the growing foetus, influencing factors at the time of birth of the baby and then during growing years, genetic and chromosomal factors that may cause developmental disabilities.

3. Case Study. In this chapter, the book now addresses the various techniques and methods of collecting information about the child with developmental disabilities like observation and interview methods, and case record proforma. The last element of this chapter is a gift to the students who are the clinicians of the future.

4. Pedigree Chart. This addition in the textbook is made with due consideration to improve the case history taking skills of students. The author highlights the understanding and difference between pedigree chart and genogram, and commonly used symbols in family tree to prepare the pedigree chart i.e. pictorial depiction of a family using symbols.

5. Psychological Report Writing. It covers the basics of the concept of report writing, providing ample information on the contents of a good report with few samples.

6. Individualized Education Programme (IEP). IEP is the most essential aspect in the education of children with exceptionality. The chapter covers the historical background of IEP, it's components, role of Psychologists and behavioral approach,

assessment for current level of functioning, goal setting, format for IEP and guidelines to fill part A and part B, lesson plan, and educational technology in India.

7. Behaviour Modification Techniques. This chapter is the middle or the bridge from disabilities to rehabilitation. Behavior modification is practical ground where the parents and individuals with developmental disabilities take a step towards making the life smoother. That is why this chapter has special value for any aspiring practitioner who wants to work in intervention. The chapter has explanation of behaviour and behaviour modification, historical background, premise of BM that covers problem behaviours, skill behaviours, steps to be followed in BM, techniques of decreasing problem behaviour and techniques of increasing skill behaviours, reinforcers and methods of selecting reinforcers and method of group rewards.

8. Sample case studies of Behaviour Modification. Readers will be able to have a proper idea of how a case taking session is conducted through sample case studies. This section aims to make the students aware of the complete process that encompasses from intake of a patient to rehabilitation, through behavior modification. These samples are basically the summation of the book chapters which are real cases taken by the author during her practice as a rehabilitation psychologist.

9. Rehabilitation. This chapter mentions the difference between habitation and rehabilitation. The need and history of rehabilitation becomes the next focus of this chapter. Rehabilitation is the process through which a person bounces back to life and lives to the optimum possible level. So, the book stresses on the importance of rehabilitation services by discussing the models of rehabilitation. Assessment and parental role in the rehabilitation remains of paramount importance, which the author has highlighted in this chapter.

10. References. This section is the foundation stone to this book, offered by researchers, clinicians, special educators; without whose pioneering work this book could not have taken shape. The students can now have the opportunity to foray into disabilities as a subject through this section.

Dr Neerja Pandey

ACKNOWLEDGEMENT

This book would not have been possible without my wonderful students for whom I have taken extensive notes in each topic that has led to the clearing of old handwritten notes, compilation and creation of this book.

The constant pestering of my friends and colleagues, which was borderline bothersome although encouraging without which I would not have thought of putting it all together. Furthermore, I am grateful to their sustained efforts in providing me platforms to write.

I take this opportunity to thank Ms. Sarika Chuni who actually made the soft copy of chapter six which is about Individualised Education Programme (IEP).

I am grateful to late Dr Anju Nagaur for taking a chance on me to write a book chapter for her which made me believe in my writing caliber. I further extend my gratitude to -

Ms. Shweta Srivastava, my friend, for trusting in me, always.

Dr. Saurabh Srivastava, my buddy, for remaining beside me and holding the light to bring clarity in my foggiest confusions.

Ms. Reetika Pal for believing in my capabilities.

Ms. Anindya S. Nag for always being enthusiastically available as a constant source of motivation and being the critique for my work.

Last but not the least and worth mentioning - my husband, Anil, who started noticing my sincere efforts at writing and made sure that I get uninterrupted time to write. Thank you, dear husband.

ABOUT THE AUTHOR

Dr. NEERJA PANDEY received PhD in Psychology from Osmania University, Telangana; MPhil in Rehabilitation Psychology from NIEPID Secunderabad, Telangana; and B.Ed. (regular) from Gorakhpur University, Uttar Pradesh. She is currently imparting her wisdom as Assistant Professor of Psychology at Amity Institute of Behavioural and Allied Sciences (AIBAS) in Amity University Lucknow Campus since 2013.

She has published research papers in psychology which include *Journey of Portrayal of Disability from Mother India to Margarita with a Straw: A Critical Review.* (Aug 2018), *Creation of Inclusive Classroom: A Conceptual Framework.* (May 2019), and many more. Her notable contribution to psychotherapy includes *'EFT as a tool to resolve anxiety: a case study approach* (July 2020)'- a topic in which she takes considerable pride in teaching and using as a psychotherapeutic tool. Her primary work in **Rehabilitation helped her write a chapter on Rehabilitation in the book titled 'Disability is not Inability – Shift Paradigm from Charity to Rights' (2021).**

Other than being registered practitioner with Rehabilitation Council of India (CRR No.: A – 10626), she is a trained Integrated Clinical Hypnotherapist, certified from EKAA Foundation as well as a past-life regression therapist from TASSO International, Netherlands. She is also the EKAA Foundation Course Facilitator along with being a life time member of 'Association of Rehabilitation Psychologists India (ARPI)'.

A supportive wife of an army officer, now retired, pillar of strength to two beautiful daughters, and a home maker, I have a zest for learning which motivated me to paint the canvas of my life with colours out of 'ordinaire'. Opportunity to travel and live in most parts of India has been advantageous. It gave me a rich knowledge, appreciation, and insight into different cultures and related issues. Being a voracious reader with eclectic interests keeps me well informed and updated.

To know more about the author:

E mail: pandeyneerja@gmail.com
LinkedIn - https://www.linkedin.com/in/dr-neerja-pandey-30241978/
Facebook page: @TheChroniclesofNeerja

1

DEVELOPMENTAL DISABILITIES – AN INTRODUCTION

People have a spectrum of abilities but at times an individual may face difficulty due to an impairment. This impairing condition compels the individual to accommodate and adapt in various ways which may help them to carry out activities of daily life. It also creates such situations in the life of the affected individual that they face restriction in gaining optimum level of functioning. The impairment could be due to the loss of functioning in a body part, or due to an abnormality in the function of a body part. It also happens due to loss of a body part or abnormality in a body part. These limitations are termed as Disability. In other words, disability is a restriction or lack of ability in comparison to the standard norm of the society. It may involve physical impairment, visual impairment, hearing impairment, intellectual disability, locomotor disability, or specific learning disability and many more. Important point is that when an individual has an impairment in any particular area of functioning, then that individual has the corresponding disability only. There need not be any other disability and that is why, it is imperative to understand that people with disability are functional in other aspects of life. For example, if an individual has visual impairment, then only the vision is affected and other senses are fully functional including their emotions. These other senses may be used to help the individual to learn innovative skills that empower them to function fully to the optimum level possible.

The disability may generate handicap for the affected individual i.e. the treatment which is meted out to this individual by the environment. For example, the individual with visual impairment does not get a chance to receive education or to receive training in certain skills that may enable him to earn for himself, or people around him tease and misbehave with him so on and so forth. At times, individuals having some or the other impairment get labeled which become stigma for them. The disability could be by birth i.e. innate or it may be acquired after birth. It may be easily visible or it may be hidden. Be it by birth or acquired later, be it visible or hidden, the impairment and subsequent disability has multidimensional effect on the individual's life, and collectively they are called Handicap. In other words, handicap refers to the process of the individual having disability being discriminated against and given disadvantage from, by and in the society, intentionally or otherwise, as a result of their disability or impairment, preventing them from actually living and leading a quality life.

Impairment and disability may be visible or invisible (as in Specific Learning Disability), it may be permanent or temporary, it may be progressive (as in Glaucoma or Duchenne Muscular Dystrophy) or regressive. Thus, a disability is defined as a condition which is significantly impaired in comparison to the standard norms. Whenever an individual has a disability, it doesn't remain as an individual issue, it becomes a family problem. Each member of the family gets affected. The hardest hit are the siblings who have no disability. Because the complete focus goes to the disabled child, so the non-disabled child may feel neglected and may develop antipathy for the disabled sibling. The parents and the care-givers feel the pressure and stress, they need counselling, support, and guidance. Thus, the concept of family counselling and community rehabilitation (covered in chapter 7).

Let us understand the meaning of related concepts.

Impairment: Impairment is loss of or abnormality in the <u>function</u> of a body part or an organ. It could also be due to <u>loss of a body part</u> or an organ.

Disability: Disability means restriction or lack of ability to perform an activity in such a manner which is considered normal for a human being and it happens due to the impairment.

Handicap: the treatment which is meted out to this individual by the environment, a disadvantage he/she faces because of the disability.

INTERNATIONAL CLASSIFICATION OF IMPAIRMENTS, DISABILITIES AND HANDICAPS (ICIDH) 1980

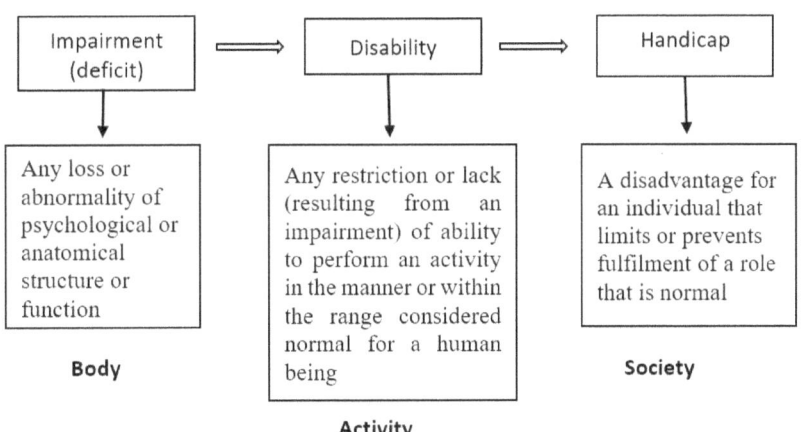

Following are some examples to differentiate between these three concepts:

1) A boy, who is 4 years of age, has mild level of cerebral palsy has stiffness in his legs due to which he cannot move his legs. So, he needs support to stand.
   - Impairment: the stiffness in his legs resulting in his inability to move his legs at the joints.

- Disability: his inability to walk is the disability which may improve with therapy and right equipment.
- Handicap: his disability does not let him live his life like any other 4-year-old either at home or at school or in the society.

2) Another 8-year-old child has extreme reading difficulty.
- Impairment: inability to associate sounds with symbols.
- Disability: inability to read.
- Handicap: failing in her grades in school due to not able to read. This may interfere in her progress in other academic areas.

ROLE OF THE INDIAN GOVERNMENT

India is the signatory of UN convention that deals with Rights of Persons with Disabilities (UNCRPD). The Convention came into effect on 3rd May 2008. Being a signatory to the Convention, India follows the guidelines given in the Convention. The PWD Act of 1995 did not have such provisions that followed the guidelines completely and so, there was the need to have a rights-based legislation with a strong institutional mechanism. The Bill was proposed by the Ministry of Social Justice and Empowerment after extensive consultation with various stakeholders, State Governments/United Territories and concerned Central Ministries and Departments. It has become the responsibility of concerned governments to give and make sure that the people with disabilities have equal rights just as any other citizen of India. The extension of network of service delivery through establishment of DDRC is one major initiative of Government of India to commence rehabilitation services at district level throughout the country. Idea behind this initiative was to converge activities of all the government departments for optimal utilization of both government as well as non-government resources to produce a synergic effect.

Disability Rehabilitation Centers (DDRC)

Hence, the Department of Empowerment of Persons with Disabilities (Divyangjan), under the Ministry of Social Justice and Empowerment (Government of India), has implemented District Disability Rehabilitation Centers (DDRC) with Disability Commissioner in each district of every Indian State. The main objective of this scheme is to provide appropriate, individual, and need-based rehabilitation services to people of all the categories of disabilities in every community.

Mental Health Act (1987)

Mental Health Act of 1987 dealt with treatment and care of people suffering with mental illness. It was about safety them safety and care especially with property and other related affairs. The Act of 1987 was emended in 2017 in which the word 'care' was added. Now it is called 'The Mental Health Care Act 2017' but the objective remained the same i.e., the people suffering with mental illness should get appropriate health-care services, protection, and promotion as and when required. Also to ensure their rights of equality.

International Classification of Functioning, Disability And Health (ICF)

The International Classification of Functioning, Disability and Health (commonly known as ICF) is an initiative of World Health Organisation (WHO) that handles the issues of health and disability at two levels, a) individual level, and b) population level. It was sanctioned by the 191 members of WHO during 2001 assembly. The member states accepted it international standard of health and disability. It originally was formed in 1980 and it was named 'International Classification of Impairments, Disabilities, and Handicaps (ICIDH)'. It was meant to provide a classification of consequences of diseases.

ICF has four classifications, one that describes functions of the body, second that describes structures of the body, third describes activities, and fourth describes participation of individuals. It also has list of environmental factors making it useful in clinical settings, health services or surveys at the individual or population level. The major components of ICF are body function and structure, activities related to an individual and his/her participation in real life situations, and environmental information.

For information on different acts on disability, one can visit the government website - http://disabilityaffairs.gov.in/content/page/acts. php. Brief introduction of the acts is being provided below.

PWD Act (1995)

Persons with Disabilities (Equal Opportunities, Protection of Rights and Full Participation) Act, 1995 (PWD Act) was in force since 1996 (when it was implemented) and it had covered all the states in India except the states of Jammu and Kashmir. The main provisions of the Act were: prevention and early detection of disabilities, free education of disabled children till age 18 with appropriate facilities, 3% reservation in Government jobs, research and man-power development, social security, and grievance cell. It had covered Blindness, low vision, leprosy-cured, hearing impairment, locomotor disability, mental retardation, and mental illness under its purview. The Act was repealed in 2016 and the new act "The Rights of Persons with Disabilities" (RPwD Act) Act, 2016 came into force. The original 7 types of disabilities have been increased 21 types of disabilities in this new Act. Moreover, the central government has retained the power to increase it number further as and when deemed fit.

RPwD Act (2016)

This new Act has emphasised one's rights – right to equality and opportunity, right to inherit and own property, right to home and family and reproductive rights among others. It also talks about accessibility - setting a two-year deadline for the government to ensure that persons with disabilities get barrier-free entry into physical infrastructure and transport systems. Additionally, it will also hold the private sector responsible including educational institutions 'recognized' by the government such as privately owned universities and colleges. One important feature is the inclusion of not just disabilities but handicaps as well.

It fulfills the obligations to the UN Convention specifically about the Rights of Persons with Disabilities (UNCRPD), to which India is a signatory. Central government has the provision to add more disabilities as and when required. The appropriate governments are responsible to take care that persons with disabilities enjoy their rights. The Act has provisions such as providing free education to children with disabilities till age 18, 5% reserved seats in government and government-aided higher educational institutes, 4% reservation in government jobs, accessibility in public buildings, to create funds for financial support to persons with disabilities, designated special courts to handle cases concerning violation of rights of PwDs and few more.

Disabilities covered under the RPwD Act are:

1. **Physical Disability**
    a) Locomotor Disability
        i)   Leprosy Cured Persons
        ii) Cerebral Palsy
        iii) Dwarfism
        iv) Muscular Dystrophy
        v)   cid Attack Victims

    b) Visual Impairment
- i)   Blindness
- ii) Low Vision

    c) Hearing Impairment
- i)   Deaf
- ii) Hard of Hearing

    d) Speech and Language Disability

2. Intellectual Disability
- a) Specific Learning Disabilities
- b) Autism Spectrum Disorder

3. Mental Behaviour (Mental Illness)

4. Disability Caused due to –
- a) Chronic Neurological Conditions such as –
  - i)   Multiple Sclerosis
  - ii) Parkinson's Disease
- b) Blood Disorder –
  - i)   Haemophilia
  - ii) Thalassemia
  - iii) Sickle Cell Disease

5. Multiple Disabilities

Along with the RPwD Act, the Department of Empowerment of Persons with Disabilities (Divyangjan) administers two more acts namely, RCI Act of 1992 and National Trust of 1999.

National Trust Act 1999

National Trust was set up for the welfare of persons with Autism, Cerebral Palsy, Mental Retardation, and Multiple Disabilities with the objective facilitating persons with disability to live independently, and to get equal opportunities. It aims at extending support to organisations registered with it. Most important function of National Trust is to evolve hassle-free procedures to appoint guardians and trustees for persons with disability especially if they outlive their parents and care-takers.

Rehabilitaion Council of India (RCI) 1992

RCI was set up as an top most body under the Ministry of Social Justice and Empowerment in 1992 and it became statutory body in 1993 to regulate and standardize the training programmes along with syllabi in disability rehabilitation. It maintains a central register of all qualified professionals working in rehabilitation and special education. It prescribes action against people who are unqualified and delivering services to persons with disability. Other functions are to prescribe minimum educational level and training of professionals and to recognise institutes and universities running professional courses in disability rehabilitation.

Unique Disability Identification (UDID)

Unique ID for Persons with Disabilities is a project of Department of Empowerment of Persons with Disabilities under the Ministry of Social Justice and Empowerment to create a national database of Persons with Disabilities (PwDs) and to issue identity cards to each PwD. Its purpose is to encourage transparency, efficiency and ease of delivering the Government benefits to PwDs, to ensure uniformity, to streamline the tracking of hierarchy of implementation from village level, block level, state level and national level. The project aims at building an integrated system to issue universal ID and disability certificates with identification and disability details.

DPNA CODE

DPNA Code stands for 'Disabled Passenger with intellectual or developmental disability Needing Assistance' a special service request code is an effort to help passengers travelling by airline with a child or an adult needing assistance. The International Air Transport Association (IATA) introduced this code in 2008. This code, used at the time of booking airline tickets, alerts the staff to special assistance needed by the concerned passenger. They know what is required to be done to assist the passenger and the family. Majority of the people travelling by air and ticket agents are not aware of the existence of this code. It is specifically applicable to IATA member airlines. Air India, Vistara, SpiceJet and Indigo IATA members from India and so they follow the DPNA Code. The code is a big relief to parents having children with Intellectual Disability, or Autism Spectrum Disorder, or Down Syndrome or any similar issue. The only condition is that the code has to be mentioned at the time of ticket booking.

REHABILITATION INITIATIVE 2030 BY WHO

The initiative was launched in February 2017 to emphasise the need to urgently take action to increase the rehabilitation efforts across nations. For this purpose, 10 specific areas have been identified namely, creation of strong leadership, strengthening rehabilitation planning and implementation, strengthening intersectoral links between, integration of rehabilitation into health sector, building rehabilitation service delivery models, developing multidisciplinary rehabilitation workforce, expanding financial support for rehabilitation, collection of relevant information about rehabilitation, building research capacity, establishing and strengthening network and partnership in rehabilitation between countries.

The upcoming chapters cover related areas such as, causes and prevention of disability, assessment in disability, Individualised Educational Programme (IEP) for children with disability, Behaviour Modification Techniques for intervention purpose, Rehabilitation, and Report writing.

- The next chapter is about potential causes of disability understanding of which helps in taking preventive measures.

The topics covered are prevention at three levels, factors that may negatively affect the growing foetus, influencing factors at the time of birth of the baby and then during growing years, genetic and chromosomal factors that may cause disability.

2

CAUSES OF DISABILITIES AND THEIR PREVENTION

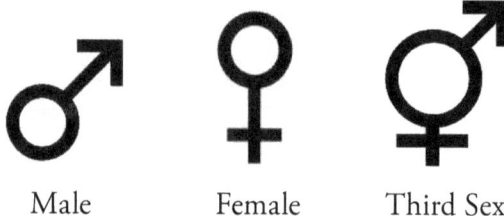

Male   Female   Third Sex

Understanding of causes of disabilities influences two major areas namely, treatment and prevention. Moreover, identification of a particular cause facilitates the treatment of the condition and also it highlights the preventive measures that are to be taken. Preventive measures do not allow the disabling condition to manifest in future generations.

Education is most effective in preventing the occurrence of disabling or handicapping conditions and hence, the inclusion of disability chapter in Psychology curriculum. Prevention happens at three levels viz. primary, secondary and tertiary.

Primary Prevention – It is the action taken before manifestation of any disease or disability. Action taken as primary prevention removes the chances of any disease or disability from getting manifested. For example, when the pregnant woman is immunized during pregnancy. It is one of the surest ways of protection for both, the mother as well as the child, from certain infections.

Secondary Prevention – It is the action that is taken immediately after identification of a disabling condition. It either stops or slows down the progress of the disease or the disability. When preventive measures are taken at initial stages of a disorder and when it prevents further complications then it is called secondary prevention. It is based on early identification and early intervention measures undertaken.

Tertiary Prevention – It is the action taken to reduce or minimize the limitations an individual faces due to an impairment. It helps in reducing the suffering of the affected individual. All the rehabilitation measures taken so that the individual achieves highest level of functioning possible, come under tertiary prevention.

The environment can affect the development before conception by influencing the sperm or the egg cell. The embryo and (later) the foetus, is vulnerable enough to get affected by a number of factors that have been explained under 'pre-natal'. Not just during the gestational period but even at the time of birth and after the birth, a baby is vulnerable to many stimulants that have influence the achievement of developmental milestones.

There are five expressions that are used in pediatrics namely, pre-natal, natal, neo-natal, peri-natal, and post-natal but, for ease of our understanding we are using only three terms, i.e., prenatal, natal and postnatal to understand influencing factors.

POINTS TO PONDER:

Pre-Natal: (from conception till before delivery)
1. Age of the expectant mother at conception: Ideally, the minimum age of expectant woman at conception of her first child should be 18 or more because it is believed that, the body is still growing and developing till 18 years of age. Even the hormonal changes are rampant till then. Female are born with all the egg cells they're ever going to have. No new egg cells are made during her lifetime. There are about 1 million eggs at birth, and around 3 lakhs at puberty. About 300 to 400 eggs

mature in the reproductive lifetime of a woman but this number differs from one woman to another.

Fertility drops as woman ages due to decrease in number and quality of remaining eggs because as older eggs divide, they become prone to errors resulting in abnormal chromosomes. So, the ideal age for pregnancy is between 18 and 35.

2. Height of the expectant mother. Studies show that short mothers generally have short pregnancies and small babies. There is also the risk of pre-mature birth.

3. LMP – Last Menstrual Period: the date of first day of last menstrual period.

4. EDD – Expected Date of Delivery: estimation of gestational age. Naegele formula – add calendar months and 7 days to last menstrual period, i.e. LMP+9 months+7 days.

   For example, the woman had her first day of last menstrual period on 1st Jan. by adding 9 calendar months it comes to 1st October. Then add 7 days i.e. 8th October which becomes EDD

5. Ante – natal checkups.
   - Once a month up to 7th month
   - Twice a month from 7th to 9th month
   - Once a week after 9th month

6. Number of pregnancies. More number of pregnancies affect the physical and mental health of the mother.

7. Number of miscarriages also affect the overall health of the woman. Moreover, reason for miscarriage is very important. Dilation & Curettage (D&C) is required for cleaning of the uterus by a gynaecologist so that there is no further complications.

8. Number of abortions (expulsion of foetus up to 5th month/26 weeks) - recurrent abortions: 3 or more consecutive spontaneous abortions have negative influence on the health of the woman.

9. Types of abortion:
   a) Spontaneous abortion, b) Induced abortion
      - Threatened abortion: Vaginal bleeding during 1st 20 weeks may /may not be with uterine contractions,

or when the abortion is not complete though it had begun.

- Inevitable abortion: Along with conditions of threatened abortion, the uterine contractions become increasingly painful and strong, and lead to dilation of cervix, or the situation is such that pregnancy cannot be continued.
- Incomplete abortion: the products of conception have been expelled partly (incomplete).
- Complete abortion: when the uterus is completely empty having ejected all the pregnancy material.
- Missed abortion: when the foetus is dead but has been retained inside the uterus for more than 4 weeks.
- Therapeutic abortion: the pregnancy was terminated legally for a specific medical indication.
- Criminal abortion: abortion was induced illegally for social reasons.

10. Ectopic pregnancy: The condition in which the fertilized ovum fails to reach the uterine cavity and gets implanted in some part of the fallopian tube. The implantation can occur in:
    - Some part of fallopian tube
    - Ovary
    - Abdominal cavity
11. Expectant mother's nutrition.
12. Radiation (Bhopal Gas Tragedy, Japan Leakage in Nuclear plant due to Tsunami, X – Ray, Mobile phones)
13. Exposure to toxic radiation of males one week before conception.
14. Exposure to Lead (leads to IDD) – Water, Soils
15. Goiter/Thyriod in foothills due to iodine deficiency and presence of chlorine in water
16. Medical condition of the expectant mother:
    - Hyper tension - Normal blood pressure is 120/80 mm Hg. When the blood pressure of the expectant mother is high then her blood vessels constrict and blood supply to the

foetus is less. Less oxygen supply results in a condition called Apoxia.

- <u>Diabetes</u>: It results in congenital anomalies and brain damage to the baby.
- <u>Gestational Diabetes</u>: It is detected during the pregnancy (especially during third trimester) because it is difficult for some women to endure the hormonal changes that occur during the pregnancy and they develop insulin resistance. This lack of insulin and high level of blood sugar are passed on to the foetus. Foetus starts producing more insulin to compensate and blood sugar becomes normal. But it results in enlarged organs – high weight, big heart, large heart resulting in complications during delivery like birth injury. Immediately after birth the baby is not fed, her insulin level rises very high and her blood sugar goes down producing the condition known as Hypoglycemia which causes coma, fits, or brain damage within half-an-hour. Immediate breast feeding and glucose are required to be given to the baby.

  Normal Blood glucose = more than 126 mg/decilitre on fasting;

  Normal blood sugar = 80-120mg/100L on fasting.

  For diabetic women sugar count should be 90 before conception.
- High fever (hyperthermia)
- Vaginal Bleeding
- White discharge

17. Fits (duration, frequency, medication).
18. Accident, if any.
19. Emotional trauma
20. Drugs, smoking, alcohol (Foetal Alcohol Syndrome).
21. Passive smoker
22. Polyhydramnois (more fluid in the uterus, neural-tube defect suspected) and Oligohydramnois (less fluid in the uterus, very dangerous)

23. Placenta Previa: When the placenta is implanted in the lower part of uterus. Foetus presses the placenta (the organ that connects the developing foetus to the wall of the uterus) in the 9th month. Due to weak attachment bleeding takes place resulting in less blood supply to the foetus.

24. Jaundice: Jaundice to mother due to water-borne infection resulting in Jaundice to the baby within 24 hours of birth. Baby can go in coma or still birth can happen due to very high level of bilirubin. If there is abrupt bleeding during III trimester as a result of hypertension then termination of pregnancy is must.

25. **Rh** incompatibility: Traditionally we know that we humans have four types of blood (as discovered by Karl Landstiener in 1900s) namely, A B Ab and O. The discovery of fifth kind of blood group was made in 1960s and it was named Hh or Bombay Blood group because it was first discovered in Bombay (now Mumbai). Different blood groups indicate presence of antigens, either A or B or none, on red blood cells (RBC). Blood with antigen A is called A blood group, the blood with antigen B is called B blood group, and when there is no antigen then it is called O blood group. Antigens A and B have ancestral antigen called antigen H.

Negative blood group means absence of protein Rh (derived from Rhesus monkey) in the blood and positive blood group means presence of the Rh protein. If the expectant mother's blood group is 'negative' and the foetus takes on the 'positive' blood group (genes decide what blood group the foetus will have) then at the time of delivery, positive blood of the baby may enter into the mother's bloodstream. This positive blood is foreign agent/antigen in her blood, so her body will develop antibodies which she will have in her body all her life but with no ill effect on her health whatsoever.

Now, with second pregnancy, if the foetus again has positive blood group, then the antibodies given by mother will react with blood of the foetus and kill its red blood cells. The baby will be born with jaundice, i.e. from day one baby will have jaundice. This can produce any kind of disorder in the baby.

- The mother is vaccinated with immunoglobulin either within 72 hours of baby's birth or during the pregnancy itself so that the positive blood of the foetus does not act as antigen in mother's blood because it is taken care of by the injected vaccine.

- Antibodies, also called immunoglobulins, Y-shaped molecules are proteins manufactured by the body that help fight against foreign substances called antigens. **Antigens** are those substances that stimulate the immune system to produce antibodies. Antigens can be bacteria, viruses, or fungi that cause infection and disease.

BOMBAY BLOOD:

Bombay blood is a rare blood group first detected by Dr. Bhende in Bombay, India in 1952. The Bombay blood is commonly mistaken as "O" blood. It is not easily identified due to lack of necessary technology in blood banks. Bombay blood differs from O blood type by lacking H antigen on RBCs.

When we say someone has blood group A, it implies that the person has antigen of type 'A' and antibody of type 'B' in his/her blood. People with AB have both antigen A and B in their blood and no antibodies. People with O blood group have only antibodies A and B and no antigens. However, what is not generally known is that all these groups have an antigen H on in the blood as well. There are very few people who do not have this antigen H also in their blood. Instead they have antibody H because of which no other blood can be given to them.

26. Teratogens: a drug, a chemical, an infection, or an environmental agent that, by acting during both the embryonic as well as foetal

period, alters morphology and subsequent function in the post-natal period. First trimester is very important. If mother is exposed to them then congenital anomalies take place. Diabetes is also a teratogen.

Infections (to the pregnant woman) – STORCH

S – Syphilis: sexually transmitted infection, highly contagious, simple to cure with right treatment.

T – Toxoplasmosis: a parasite through contact with cat and cattle. Transplacental (transmitted through placenta) resulting in microcephaly.

O – Others: HIV, gonorrhea (sexually transmitted infection), men get it more often than women, also called 'the clap'.

R – Rubella: or German measles, MMR vaccine is given to pregnant woman at 18 months of pregnancy. Hearing impairment is the result. Vaccine is given to the woman and advised to conceive after minimum 1 year but only after getting medical checkup done.

C – Cytomegalovirus: a kind of herpesvirus which usually produces very mild symptoms in an infected person but may cause severe neurological damage in people with weak immune systems and in the new born. It affects the brain and common resultant is CP. At times, microcephaly is also the resultant.

H – Herpes simplex virus: sexually transmitted, transferred through vagina at birth. Developmental delay takes place, caesarean section is done. Rashes and skin problems to mother.

Natal (during birth and around birth):

Sexually transmitted diseases can be contracted by the foetus during the trip through the vagina at the time of birth.

1. Full Term Normal Delivery (FTND). Delivery is termed normal if it fulfils the following criteria:
   - Spontaneous onset at term (no use of forceps or vacuum or any other assistance)
   - It is with vertex presentation
   - It is without undue prolongation
   - Natural expulsion of the foetus with minimal aids (incision on the vagina i.e. *chhota* operation)
   - When delivery is without any complications
2. Labour (13 to 14 hours with first child): Labour is a chain of events that take place in the genital organs of the woman so that the baby can be expelled out of the womb through the vagina into the outer world.
3. Stages of labour:
   - First stage: starts with onset of true labour and ends with full dilation of the cervix.
   - Second stage of labour: starts with full dilation of the cervix (not from rupture of membranes) and ends with expulsion of the foetus from birth canal.
   - Third stage: begins after expulsion of the foetus and ends with expulsion of the placenta and membranes.
4. Gestational period (full term is from 37 to 42 weeks)
5. Delivery: expulsion or extraction of viable/live foetus out of the womb, not synonymous with labour. Delivery can take place without labour as an elective caesarean section.
6. Place of delivery (it includes travel and, in the bathroom, due to enema)
7. Type of delivery:
   - Normal
   - Caesarean section

- Forceps (assisted delivery)
- Vacuum (assisted delivery)

8. What happened immediately before delivery.
   Position of the foetus in the womb (foetal position)
   - Breech presentation: either buttocks or legs come out first
   - Transverse presentation: hands come out first
   - Vertex presentation: head comes out first, back side
   - Face presentation: face facing downward
   - Prolapsed cord: umbilical cord comes out first
   - Dry labor: fluid comes out first
   - Cord around the neck
   - Caul baby: baby comes out with the sac

9. Delivered child:
   - irth cry (within 5 minutes of birth)
   - Birth weight (2.5 kg to 3.8 kg by Indian standard)
   - Birth colour (blue/pink)
   - Head circumference (30 cm)
   - Weight of the brain (350 gram in new born, 1200-1400 grams in adults)

APGAR Score: The Apgar score is a scoring system doctors and nurses use to assess newborns at one minute and five minutes after they're born. Dr. Virginia Apgar created the system in 1952. It is taken immediately after birth in the labour room. It is taken at 1st minute, at 3rd minute, and at 5th minute after birth. Scoring ranges from 1 to 10. (A score of 8-10 is normal, score of 0-3 at fifth minute indicates neurological problems, 6-8 is at risk baby, and below 6 means brain damage).

A – Appearance (colour)
P – Pulse (heart beat (120-140/sec for neonate)
G – Grimace (reflex) – response to stimuli
A – Activity (muscle tone and movement of limbs)
R – Respiration (breathing with or without effort)

10. Fever

11. Pathological Jaundice (due to Rh incompatibility)
12. Physiological Jaundice (Hyperbilirubinemia): Jaundice to mother due to water borne infection resulting in jaundice to the baby after birth and/or Athetosis due to which the baby can go in coma or still birth can take place due to very high level of bilirubin.
13. Fits to the baby (if yes then its duration, number of times it occurred, and intervention done).

Post Natal: (after delivery of the baby)

1. Vaccination of the baby
2. Nutrition of the baby
3. Feeding:
   - Did not take mother's milk
   - Mother did not have milk
   - Milk could not be digested by the baby
4. Accident, if any, like slipping down from the hand of the caregiver.
5. Infection.
6. Fits (duration, frequency, treatment)

Other Causes:

1) GENETIC DISORDERS OR CHROMOSOMAL DISORDERS:

Three types of genetic disorders are:
   a) Single Gene Disorders – Dominant gene disorder, Recessive gene disorder, and X linked disorder.
   • Dominant gene - A gene may become abnormal or it may mutate itself as a result of some change in its DNA structure. If the abnormal gene is able to produce a clinical abnormality in presence of its normal counterpart, then it is a dominant gene. The trait which is expressed in F1 generation is dominant

trait & the masked one is recessive. Chances of passing of the dominant gene to the next generation is 50%.

Fragile X syndrome/ Martin-Bell syndrome is one example. This condition is inherited in an X-linked dominant pattern. Men get the symptoms more often than women. Because fathers cannot pass on the X-linked traits to their sons so, mothers become the carriers.

- Recessive gene - Recessive disease/disorder is caused by the presence of two abnormal genes inherited from both parents. In general, one recessive gene doesn't an abnormality if its counterpart is normal. We all are carriers of several abnormal recessive genes which cause no ill effect. If both parents carry the same abnormal gene then there is 25% risk or 1 in 4 chances in each pregnancy for the offspring to inherit the disorder (double dose). Consanguineous couples are at increased risk to have a child affected with recessive disorder. Risk increases with closeness of the relationship.

  Sickle cell anemia is inherited in an autosomal recessive pattern. Both the parents of an individual with an autosomal recessive condition carry one copy of the mutated gene though they do not have symptoms of the condition.

- X linked disorders - Also called sex-linked disorders involve mutant genes located on X or female sex chromosome. Affect males as males have only one X chromosome. A single dose of abnormal recessive gene can cause disease. As females have two X chromosomes, a single mutant gene should not cause a disease provided the second gene is normal. Around 400 X linked diseases are passed between generation by carrier mothers.
  - Hemophilia (Bleeder's disease) is one of them. Males are affected and females are carriers because it is linked to X chromosome recessive pattern. The characteristic feature of

X linked inheritance is that, fathers cannot pass on X-linked traits to their sons.

- Duchenne Muscular Dystrophy (DMD). It is a genetic disorder in which muscles of the body degenerate progressively. It happens due to abnormality in the protein called *dystrophin*. This protein helps in keeping the muscles intact.

b) Multifactorial - Multifactorial Inherited Disorders are caused by additive effects of both genetic as well as environmental factors (pre & postnatal conditions). The mechanism is not completely understood at present especially with regard to which environmental factors play a role & how they exert their effect. Advances in understanding of genetic defects have led to genetic counseling.

c) Chromosomal - The chromosomes get set in pairs according to standard pattern. The events that affect a child's development can occur during the cell division. When chromosomes divide unequally the cells don't survive. But when they do, they cause chromosomal abnormalities. Chromosomal disorders occur due to three types of errors numerical error, structural error and sex chromosomal abnormalities.

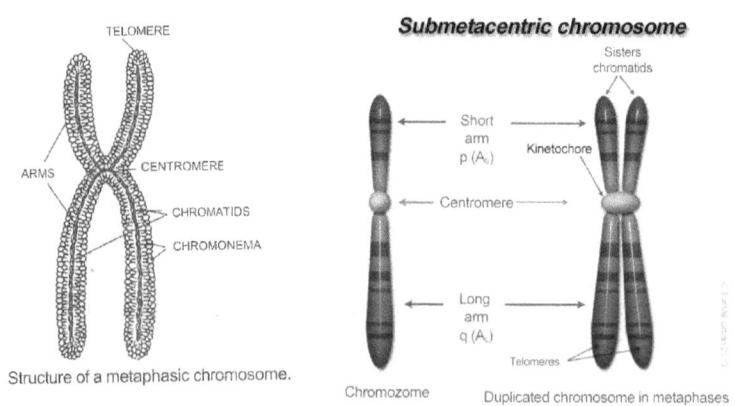

Structure of a metaphasic chromosome.

Submetacentric chromosome

Dr Neerja Pandey

NUMERICAL ERRORS - During cell division a pair of chromosomes does not split resulting in one daughter cell with 47 chromosomes (trisomy) & the other with 45 chromosomes (monosomy).

Some examples are: Down's Syndrome. Edward's Syndrome. Patau Syndrome. Turner's Syndrome, monosomy.

STRUCTURAL ERRORS - A chromosome's structure can be altered in several ways. It results from chromosome breakage and followed by reconstitution in an abnormal combination. Some of the structural re-arrangements are:

a) Deletion - A small part of the chromosome gets deleted. Some examples are cri-du-chat syndrome, Microcephaly, Prader-Willi Syndrome, Angelman Syndrome

b) Ring - A part of the chromosome breaks off to form a ring/circle like structure. The ring formation may or may not result in loss of genetic material.

c) Translocation - Part of one chromosome detaches itself and gets attached to another chromosome. In one type of translocation, portions of two chromosomes interchange and get attached with each other. In second type of translocation, the entire chromosome (both long as well as short arm) gets attached to another chromosome from the center i.e., at the centromere.

d) Isochromosome - Centromere of the chromosome divides transversely (horizontally) instead of longitudinally. One arm is missing and the other arm is duplicated.

e) Insertion - A part of the chromosome gets deleted to get attached onto the arm of another chromosome.

f) Inversion - One part of the chromosome breaks off and then it turns upside down to get reattached to the arm of the chromosome but the genetic material is reversed.

g) Duplication - portion of the chromosome is duplicated, resulting in extra genetic material.

SEX CHROMOSOMAL ABNORMALITIES –

Trisomy of sex chromosomes:
- Klinefelter Syndrome: 47 XXY, males or XXY syndrome is a condition where human male has two or more X chromosomes.
- 47XXX syndrome / super woman syndrome: in this condition the human female has three X chromosomes
- 47 XYY syndrome / Supermale syndrome: a human male inherits an extra Y chromosome

Monosomy of sex chromosomes:
- Monosomy X, Turner Syndrome – 45 X, is a condition where human female has one X chromosome and no Y chromosome
- Hermaphroditism:

Lyon hypothesis (X-inactivation)

According to the Lyon hypothesis, 1 of the 2 X chromosomes in each female somatic cell is inactivated genetically early in embryonic life (on or about day 16). In fact, no matter how many X chromosomes are present, all but 1 are inactivated. However, molecular genetic studies have shown that some genes on the inactivated X chromosome (or chromosomes) remain functional, and these few are essential to normal female development. *XIST* is the gene responsible for inactivating the genes of the X chromosome, producing RNA that triggers inactivation.

CONSANGUINITY - The word consanguineous marriage or relationship between two who have blood relation. It indicates human inbreeding and is one of the causes of genetic disorders. Consanguinity results in the inheritance from common ancestors of both parents. In some communities, consanguineous marriages between relatives are very common especially between first cousins.

Few related terms to know:
1. SGA – small for gestational period
2. LGA – large for gestational period
3. AGA – adequate for gestational period
4. IUGR – intra uterine growth retardation
5. Oxytocin – for induction of labor
6. Microcephaly – small head (less than 2 SD; +-33cm being normal)
7. Anterior Fontanelle (AF) – an opening in the skull on top of the head which closes by the age of about one and half years
8. Hydrocephaly – enlarged head due to accumulation of cerebrospinal fluid (CSF). With closed AF the head won't increase but increased fluid will put pressure.
9. VP Shunt – Ventriculoperitoneal Shunt. Insertion of a pipe/ passage between the ventricles and the peritoneum for the excess fluid to drain. It is done for hydrocephaly.

- The next chapter is about assessment using Case Study Method. It covers the concept of assessment, strengths and limitations of case study, observation and interview methods, and case record proforma.

3

CASE STUDY

Assessment is a continuous process that helps in guiding the progress of an individual. For this purpose, information is gathered from varied sources like observation of the individual, interview of the individual or the care givers (as may be the case), diaries and personal notes (if available), and result of tests and questionnaires. This whole process of gathering information from different sources is called Case Study or Case Intake. Once the study gets over then the information so gathered is written in a format. This written document is called Case History. Case History then becomes a legal document.

The in-depth information can be gathered for an individual, or a group, or an event, or a community. But in Psychology, case study is generally confined to the study of an individual for the purpose of determining the cause of the problem and for planning appropriate treatment strategies. Moreover, the focus remains on the individual (past events as well as present situation) and there is no comparison with anyone whatsoever.

Its better if only psychologists, therapists, or psychiatrists take case study because they are trained professionals. They are trained in not only asking appropriate questions using appropriate words but also in taking note of what the client does not say. They are trained in observing the bodily clues of the client and how the client answers questions. Hence, the need that a person qualified for diagnosis and treatment takes a formal case study.

STRENGTHS OF CASE STUDY
- Case study is qualitative and biographical in nature.
- It can continue for longer duration.
- The complete focus is on the individual.

- Analysis is descriptive in nature.
- Details collected are of high level.
- It combines both the objective as well as subjective data.
- It provides an in-depth understanding of the subjective experiences and corresponding perception of the concerned individual.

LIMITATIONS OF CASE STUDY

- Cause-and-effect relationship cannot be ascertained.
- Factors that affect the outcome cannot be controlled.
- The results are of limited generality because if one person behaves in certain way doesn't mean that all people would behave the same way.
- The data obtained may be second-hand in nature & so distorted by time.
- Final conclusions may reflect personal bias of the investigator.

OBSERVATION

Observation is the oldest method used by man in scientific investigation. It refers to watching & listening to the behaviour of other persons without manipulating & controlling it. Then record the findings in ways that allow some degree of analytical interpretation & discussion. It might involve watching a family during meals, monitoring school children in playground, or ask people to keep track of every hostile remark made during the day. Today observation is a perfect method of social investigation and probably the most popular one in gaining knowledge of social phenomenon.

PURPOSE OF OBSERVATION
a) Capture & study behaviour as it actually happens.
b) Observe the behaviour that cannot be replicated in experimental setting.

TYPES OF OBSERVATION

1) Participant Observation. Observer actively participates in the activities of the group under study. He / she may already be a member of the group under observation. The role of the observer may be known to the group members. Or he/she may remain disguised.

2) Non – Participant Observation. The observer does not actively participate in the activities of the group but observes them in a natural setting from a distance. He / she is able concentrate upon a specified aspect of behaviour in a better way.

3) Controlled Observation. It involves a systematic observation in controlled environment. Here the environment & stimuli are so arranged as to increase the probability of occurrence of the target behaviour. This increases the cost efficiency of the assessment method. The control is of two types namely, control over phenomena / an event and Control over observation.

Techniques Of Control
- Hypothesis formation
- Detailed observation plan.
- Use of Schedules.
- Use of mechanical devices.
- Team Observation.
- Use of a control group.

4) Non-Controlled Observation. Observations are made in natural surroundings where the activities are performed in their natural settings and in their usual course. The Observer visits the natural environment of the observed individual & record the occurrence pre-selected & pre-defined behaviour.

METHODS OF RECORDING OBSERVATIONAL DATA
- Diary description
- Specimen Description Behavior Recording
- Time Sampling

- Event Sampling
- Trait Rating - Rating scales may be used to qualify and quantify behavior. They provide accuracy to the description of behavior whether qualitative or quantitative. The more points on the scale the more scientific the description.

Never	Sometimes	Always	No participant	Avg. participants	High
0	1	2	0	1	0

- Check Lists - A prepared list of items which records the presence or absence of a certain behavior e.g., Responsibility

a) Doing homework	Yes/No
b) Placing things accurately	Yes/No
c) Taking care of belongings etc.	Yes/No

INTERVIEW

Interview method involves personal & face-to-face contact between the interviewer & the respondent with the intention of eliciting desired information from the latter. The interviewer needs to ask questions as well as observe the behaviour of the respondent to get correct information. The respondent also tries to size-up the interviewer. The inference thus drawn about the interviewer influences his/her answers.

TYPES OF INTERVIEWS

1) Formal Interview- also referred to as structured/patterned interview.

   - Already prepared questions are asked in a set order by the interviewer & answers are recorded in a standardized form. Is gaining popularity.
   - It is a systematic procedure for collecting information regarding the respondents.
   - Reported validity is usually higher than the that for informal interviews.
   - Relatively less trained interviewers can also conduct it smoothly as the whole procedure is structured.

2) Informal Interview- also called unstructured interview.

   - No pre-determined questions.
   - No pre-set order of questions.
   - It is left to the interviewer to ask some questions in his/her own way regarding key points around the interview for it to build up.
   - Situation remains unstructured.
   - Is flexible method of collecting data.
   - Interviewer gets deeper understanding of respondents' behaviour.

Clinical Interview is a type of informal interview in which the therapist asks questions to the client or the caregivers to get information.

LIMITATIONS OF INTERVIEW

   - Procedure of formal interview is expensive.
   - In informal interview there is greater scope of personal influence & bias of the interviewer.
   - Informal interview requires greater skill on the part of the interviewer.
   - Interviewer needs to be tactful, intelligent, have social sense & a deeper knowledge of subject-matter.

- Respondents are free to answer so their responses may be unreliable.
- Personality of the interviewer may influence the responses.

Case Record Proforma

[As developed by National Institute for Empowerment of People with Intellectual Disability, NIEPID (earlier NIMH), Secunderabad in Telangana State]

The Case Record, till 3.4, is common for any case intake. After pedigree chart, the information collected will depend upon the area of disability and age of the client. So, we find case studies covering different areas of investigation as per the need.

Section I

Identification Data (Case)

1.1 Name _____	0.1 Date _____
1.2 Age _____	0.2 Regn. No. _____
1.3 Sex _____	0.3 Informant _____
1.4 Education _____	0.4 Ref. by _____
1.5 Occupation _____	0.5 Language Spoken _____
1.6 Religion _____	0.6 Birth Oder _____

P.S. – *Date of birth must be asked because if the subject is below the age of 15 then it would be needed for calculation of Social Age (SA), Social Quotient (SQ), Developmental Age (DA), and Developmental Quotient (DQ). Moreover, some congenital diseases manifest after certain age e.g., muscular dystrophy starts after age 8 and in case of leukosdystrophy (of white matter) the child will be absolutely normal till first year of life and will survive upto only 4 years' of age. Plus, D.O.B helps keeping track of age in further sessions as well.*

Section II

Demographic Data (Parents/Guardians)

2.1 Father's Name   : _____

2.2 Father's Education   : _____

2.3 Father's Occupation : _____

2.4 Mother's Name   : _____

2.5 Mother's Education : _____

2.6 Mother's Occupation

2.7 Address

Local   : _____

_____

_____

_____

Permanent   : _____

_____

_____

_____

1.8 Monthly Income :_____

P.S. – *Information regarding the education of parents is required for intervention programme. Information of religion is also important as it reveals the child-rearing practices and helps in intervention. We need to respect the religion and proceed according to its practices.*

Section III

3.1 Presenting Complaints (Verbatim)

_____

_____

_____

_____

_____

3.2 History (Pre-natal, Natal, Post-natal) covered in previous chapter

_____

_____

_____

_____

_____

P.S. – *Refer Chapter 2 'Causes & Prevention of Disability'*

3.3 Family History

_____

_____

_____

_____

_____

P.S. – *Consanguinity; type of family i.e., nuclear, joint, extended; history of disability like MR, MI, Fits, or any other; significant others i.e., care givers; socio-economic status; family pathology; marital discord, etc.*

3.4 Pedigree Chart/Genogram/Family Tree (Refer chapter 4)

3.5 Developmental History Age at which attained

a) Neck Holding (2-6 months) _____

b) Sitting (5-10 months) _____

c) Walking (9-14 months) _____

d) First words (7-12 months) _____

e) Two word phrases (16-30 months _____

f) Sentences (3-4 years) _____

g) Toilet control (3-4 years) _____

h) Monetory transaction (Yes/No)

i) Avoids simple hazards (Yes/No)

j) Problems in school/Scholastic Backwardness (Yes/No)

k) Physical Deformity (Yes/No)

l) Sensory Impairment (Yes/No)

m) Fits (Yes/No)

3.6 School History

_____

_____

_____

_____

_____

P.S. – *Age of the child when first went to school and the class admitted into; type of school (normal, special, integrated, inclusive); performance at school (as reported by teacher); change of school, if any (reason, shifted to which type of school and at what age to which class); complaints, if any, by teachers and peers; playmates (older, younger, same age)*

3.7 Occupational History

_____

_____

_____

_____

_____

P.S. – *All kinds of work/help the child does at home; all kinds of work done outside home.*

3.8 Behaviour Problems, if any

_____

_____

_____

_____

_____

P.S. – *Each problem like nail biting, pencil chewing, head banging, crying, shouting, etc.*

Section IV

Assessments

4.1 Motor

_____

_____

_____

_____

_____

P.S. – *Eye-hand coordination; fine motor skills (palmer, princer, tripod grasps).*

4.2 Self Help

_____

_____

_____

_____

_____

P.S. – *Eating: indicates hunger/thirst, verbally or otherwise; Drinks water with/without spilling; mixes food or not, if knows how much food is needed; picks up food with/without support. Toilet: indication, pulling down the knickers, wearing back the clothes, washing with/without support. Brushing: with/without verbal prompting; if paste has to be applied; if can open the tap. Bathing: pours water; scrubbing (if needs help); drying with towel; holding &using soap. Grooming: combing; applying powder, oil, cream etc; wearing slippers in right way.*

4.3 Communication

_____

_____

_____

_____

_____

P.S. – *indicates needs verbally/non-verbally/with questions. Follows one/ two or more instructions. Receptive and expressive. Is able to carry out conversation. Gives appropriate answers.*

4.4 Academics

_____

_____

_____

_____

_____

P.S. – *Shows body parts, colours, and shapes. Is able to match, name or identify colours (which colour if at all). Numbers: repeat, write, count, calculate. Identification of money, difference between coins. Difference between objects. Understands days, weeks, months, date etc. Reads & writes: alphabet, & numbers, words and sentences.*

4.5 Socialization

_____

_____

_____

P.S.- *Likes to play with older children or prefers to stay alone. Recognizes family members, relatives, neighbours, & so on. Goes to neighbourhood and comes back. Age-appropriate social norms – greetings, interaction etc. Understands social situations like gatherings at someone's place, at own house, public places like temple etc.*

4.6 Educational Status

4.7 Vocational Status

P.S. – *If below 18 years of age and not in a job then put 'dash' otherwise performance in job, income and promotion. Change of job, frequency of change and duration of holding one job. If is holding the same job for a long time.*

Section V

Intellectual/Psychological Assessment
[Based on observation during the assessment]

a) General Appearance

_____

_____

_____

P.S. – *physically looks age appropriate (lean, thin, obese)*

b) General behaviour during assessment

_____

_____

_____

P.S. – *Cooperates, persistence on a task, fingering things, gives same type of answers in same style, maintains eye contact, is violent/withdrawal.*

c) Attention and concentration

_____

_____

_____

P.S. - *How is attention aroused e.g, by the name repeatedly; span of attention; sustenance of attention (e.g. for the required time)*

d) Activity Level

_____

_____

_____

P.S. – *Sluggish, active, over-active; withdrawn; not interested in doing anything.*

e) Comprehension

_____

_____

_____

P.S. – *Follows 1/2 step instructions; comprehends cold, hunger, thirst, etc; follows the steps of the test.*

f) Emotionality and behaviour

_____

_____

_____

P.S. – *Appropriateness of emotions, doesn't express any emotion, excessive crying or laughing.*

g) Relationship within/outside family (Significant stressors)

_____

_____

_____

P.S. – *If over-dependent on mother; if mother is over-protective; mother-child relationship during the assessment.*

h) Psychological tests used

_____

_____

_____

P.S. – *Purpose of testing – to assess social developmental level and mental development; language used; tests done; test result; explanation of why one of them is high (whichever has the higher score e.g., due to school and more exposure better SQ); in social age, explanation about which self-help area the subject has low score and in which high.*

i) Any other information

_____

_____

_____

j) Further testing (If required)

_____

_____

5.1 Provisional Diagnosis

_____

_____

_____

_____

P.S. – *Overall impression; based on behaviour and clinical observations, parental interview, and psychological tests the child is -------*

6.1 Management Plan

_____

_____

_____

_____

_____

P.S. – *Counseling of parents regarding the level of the child and what she can do, what she is capable doing e.g., the child may need special educational intervention depending on age, or she may need a therapy --- to deal with ---(depending on the condition)*

<u>Signatures</u>

Students:

Consultant:

Date:

Organizations dealing with any particular disability make changes in the format as per their requirement but sections I and II remain same.

CLASSIFICATION AND DEGREE OF INTELLECTUAL DISABILITY (ID)		
Category	**IQ**	**Degree of Disability**
Genius	Above 150	
Superior/Gifted	130-150	
Above Average	110-130	
Average	90-110	

Borderline	70-90	25%
Mild	50-70	50%
Moderate	35-50	75%
Severe	20-35	90%
Profound	Below 20	100%

DEGREES OF IMPAIRMENT IN HEARING IMPAIRMENT (HI)	
Category	**Threshold in decibel**
Slight	16 dB – 25 dB
Mild	26 dB – 40 dB
Moderate	41 dB – 55 dB
without amplification	56 dB -70 dB
Severe	71 dB – 90 DB
Profound	< 91 dB

CLASSIFICATION OF VISUAL IMPAIRMENT (VI)			
SNELLEN VA	VA (LogMAR)	CATEGORY	CLASSIFICATION
≥ 6/18	0.0 -0.50	0	Mild or no VI
< 6/8 – 6/60	0.52 – 1.0	1	Moderate
< 6/60 – 3/60 (6/120)	1.02 – 1.30	2	Severe
< 3/60 – 1/60	1.32 – 1.80	3	Blindness
< 1/60 - LP	1.82 – 3.0	4	Blindness
NLP	4.0	5	Blindness
Moderate and severe VI constitute low vision. VA-Visual Acuity; LogMAR-logarithm of minimum angle of resolution; LP-light perception; NLP-no light perception			

- Highlights of the next chapter is an understanding of difference between pedigree chart and genogram, and commonly used symbols to prepare the pedigree chart i.e. pictorial depiction of a family using symbols.

Dr Neerja Pandey

4

PEDIGREE CHART

Pedigree Chart is a pictorial depiction of a family, ideally, up to three generations. It is a family tree that contains information about the family lineage, and about physical and mental health of the family members.

Though the terms pedigree chart, family tree and genogram are used inter-changeably but there is a slight difference between these terms. Family tree showcases only the lineage whereas, genogram highlights the interpersonal and emotional relationships between the family members, and Pedigree Chart depicts health related information. In relationship counselling and family therapy we prepare genogram, and in the field of disability, we prepare a pedigree chart.

So, in simpler terms, we draw the family tree of the index-person, the client or the informant. Then based on the purpose, it becomes either a genogram or a pedigree chart. For example, the diagram below depicts consanguineous marriage (marriage in blood relation/marriage within the family members related with blood) in a pedigree chart but same diagram acquires a different meaning in a genogram. It indicates strong emotional bond according to genogram.

The pedigree chart uses certain symbols which have been explained in this chapter. In the pedigree chart, only the age of the individuals is mentioned, also the age at which an individual died. Rest of the information goes in the Index written at the bottom of the chart, even the cause of the death. Different marks are made inside the symbols to highlight health issues. What health issue the marks highlight is mentioned in the index. An arrow mark points to the index person or the client or whoever is the informant because family tree thus prepared is of that person. The siblings are drawn from oldest to youngest if possible. While drawing a couple, either the male or the female can be drawn on the left side. For example, if the male is drawn on the left, then the same pattern should ideally be followed in all the drawings.

SYMBOLS

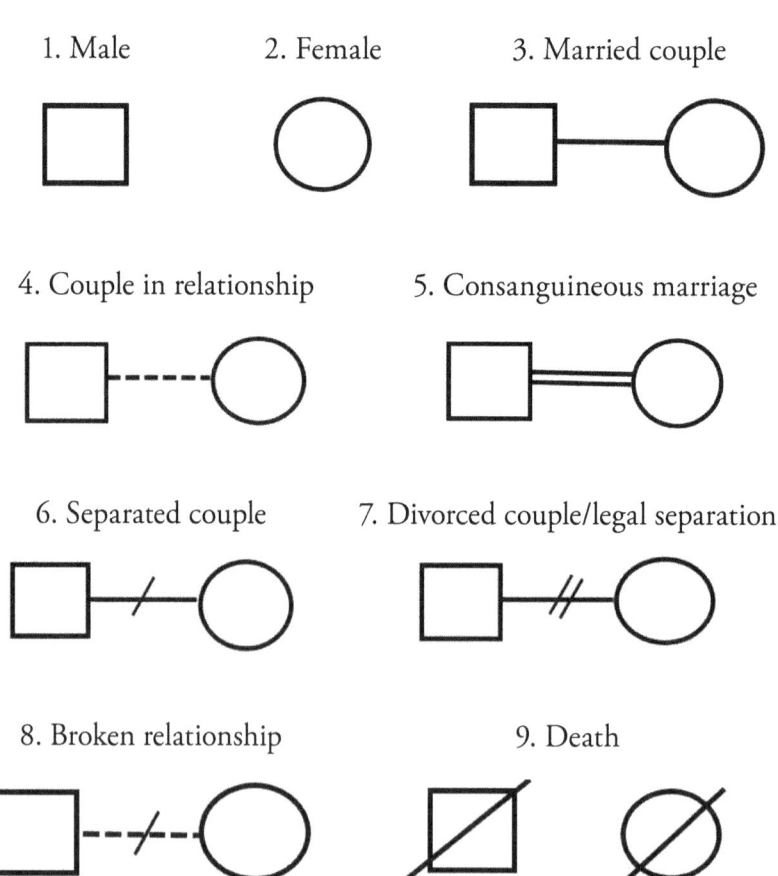

1. Male   2. Female   3. Married couple

4. Couple in relationship   5. Consanguineous marriage

6. Separated couple   7. Divorced couple/legal separation

8. Broken relationship   9. Death

10. Couple with no children

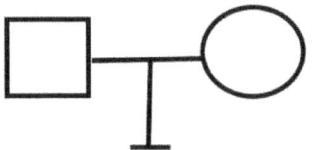

11. No children due to infertility

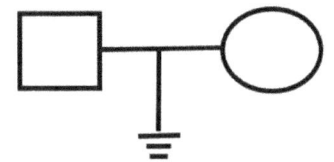

12. Pregnancy-sex not known

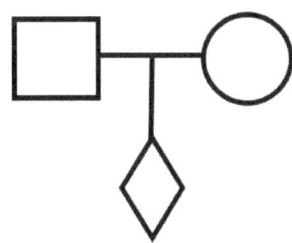

13. Two wives, both siblings

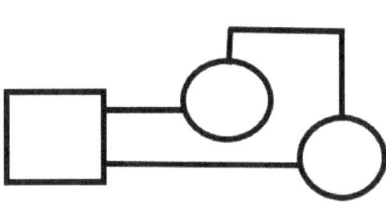

14. Two wives, one consanguineous

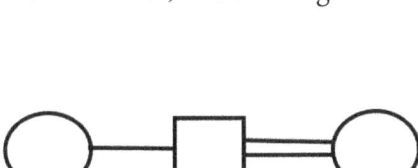

15. Siblings

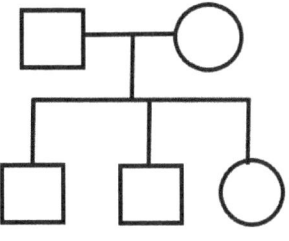

16. Identical/Monozygotic Twins

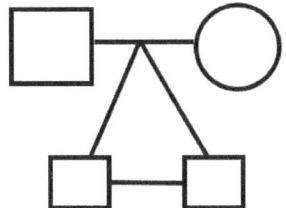

17. Fraternal/Dizygotic Twins

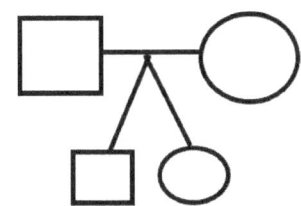

18. Adoption: a. Adoption due to infertility b. Adoption from within the family c. Adoption from outside family

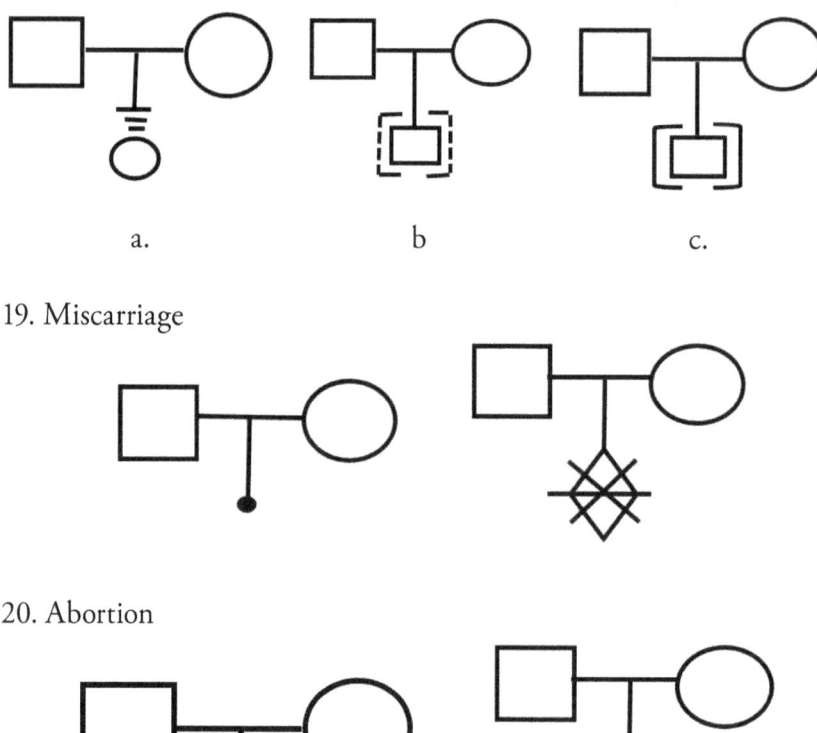

19. Miscarriage

20. Abortion

21. Still-born male child Stillborn Female child

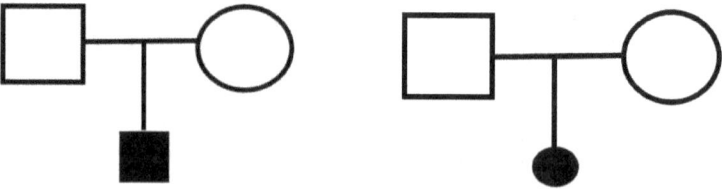

Dr Neerja Pandey

22. Sperm donor Sperm donor due to infertility

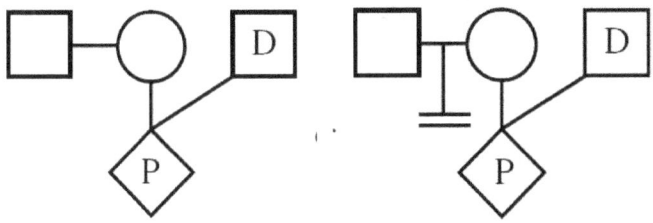

23. Ovum donor

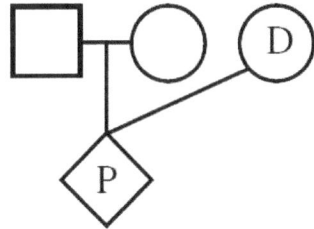

24. 1ˢᵗ degree of consanguinity with 50% genetic material transfer

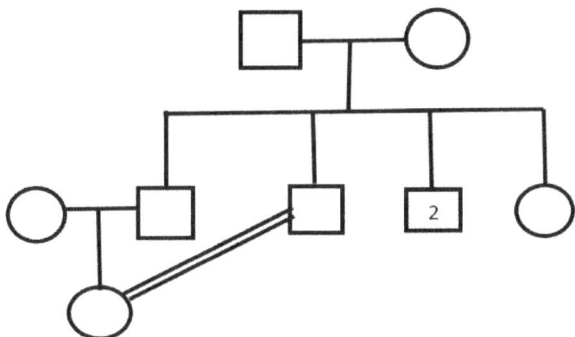

25. 2nd degree of consanguinity with one-fourth genetic material transfer

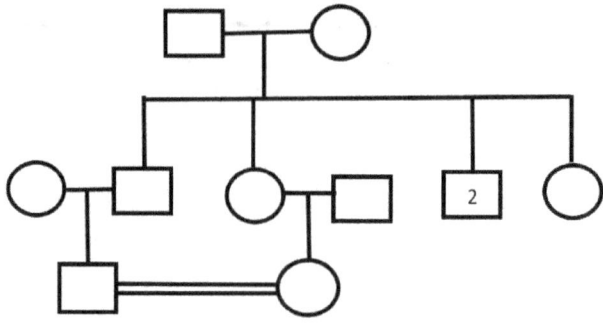

26. 3rd degree of consanguinity with one-eighth genetic material transfer

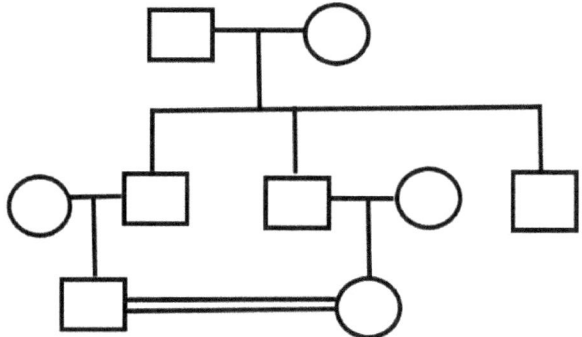

27. A hypothetical family tree in which there is one miscarriage in second generation. One abortion and one adoption in third generation.

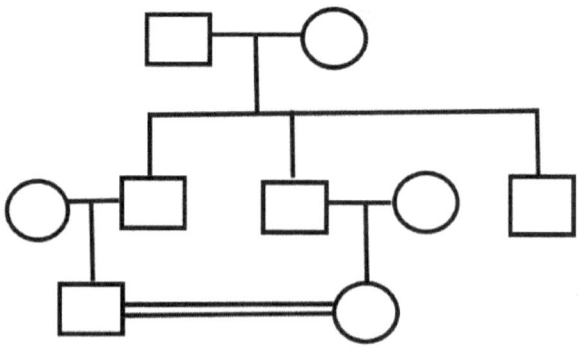

28. Case Study of a female

Index person is an ambitious female whose widowed mother remarried her own brother-in-law. The index person separated from live-in relationship from which she had one son and one daughter who died at age 22. Both the children grew up with maternal grandparents. The Index person then divorced her first husband from whom she had one daughter. This younger daughter grew up with her father. She remarried a divorcee with two sons. The elder son was in relationship with her eldest daughter. Later she divorced her second husband as well.

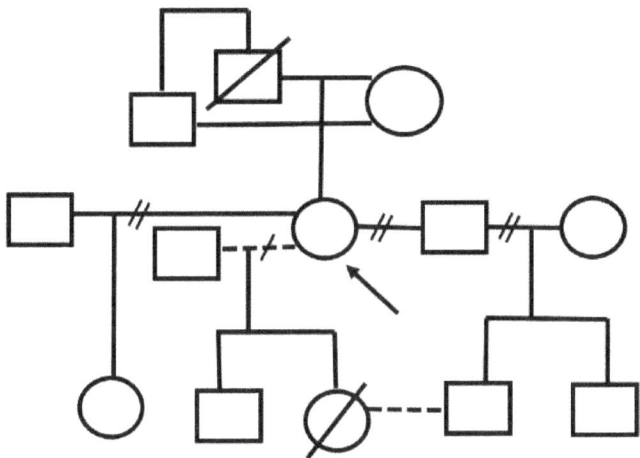

- Next chapter is on Psychological Report Writing that is the final step after assessment and the first step before starting with management programme. The chapter covers the concept of report writing, contents of a good report, and few samples.

5

PSYCHOLOGICAL REPORT WRITING

Once the assessment is over, then the report is made based on which further action is planned and executed. This report helps the therapist as well as the client/child or their care-takers to take an informed decision regarding line of treatment and therapy.

There is no one standard form, outline, or format that is followed uniformly in writing a Psychological Report. It is basically the culmination of the assessment process. Both the content as well as the style should and do vary with the purpose of the case study, context in which it is conducted, the recipients to whom the report is addressed, and theoretical orientation and professional background of the therapist. It is important to adapt the report according to the need, interest and background of those who will receive the report because the purpose of report writing is to communicate and not to obfuscate i.e. to make something less clear and more difficult to understand.

A report presents only facts, realistic picture of the client in interaction with his/her environment, personality make-up and level of functioning, and information that is written for specific readers in such a way that it may be easily scanned and understood. It has recommendations, and tables and graphs wherever needed. Conclusion of the final report is based on observation of the client by the therapist at the time of assessment, information provided to the therapist by the parents or caregivers, and the result of test/s conducted.

No matter what kind of report is being prepared, it is better to analyse before preparing it. It means, answering the following questions:
- what is the purpose of the report?
- who has asked for the report?

- how and where will the report be used?
- what should be its length, and what are the recommendations of the report?

A GOOD PSYCHOLOGICAL REPORT

The report helps to organize and clarify the therapist's own thinking about the case. It is useful for other therapists also who may evaluate the child who already has been previously seen by a psychologist.

Psychological report presents the picture of the client in three different dimensions:

a. Where the client/child has been – anything significant in the background or development, significant elements of family history or any specific information about the background.

b. Where the client/child is at present – formal test data and personality analysis. It gives an image of the client as anyone knowing and working with her would describe her.

c. What options exist for the client in future – report provides recommendations that can be useful for those who are going to be in contact with the client.

Few more points to be considered while writing a report so that it becomes a good report: -

1. Determination of primary readers because the content and the language are dependent on them. Different readers require different reports for example, only the test scores are of little value to the parents but for professionals they are of potential use.

2. Description of nature of assessment tool/s when writing for parents because it is safe to assume that they have little or no knowledge of the tests used. A small description of the sub-tests is useful. Example, instead of writing that the child is weak in coding (WISC III), it is better to write that, 'The child had a

weakness on a test that needed pencil to copy as many geometric symbols as possible in a span of 2 minutes. The symbols follow a code that are written at the top of the page.'

3. Headings and lists serve to enhance the clarity of communication. Too much information written in paragraphs lose the impact. So, additional headings can be used if any section stretches for more than a page. Lists add impact to the statement/s.

4. First paragraph or two should clearly state how the child came to be examined, who are the significant people involved, and the rout of the referral. It should also include the concern of parents, school staff, or any other significant adult in the child's life.

5. Use of child's name is always better. Instead of writing, "The child was restless during the assessment" better would be "Sandesh was restless during the assessment."

6. Clarification of meaning of certain words to ensure accuracy because there is general disagreement as to the meanings of particular words. This can be done by using examples of the child's behaviour. It benefits the psychologist as well because if the psychologist writes that a child is anxious but cannot think of a behaviour to support this statement then this conclusion should not be drawn. That's how the psychologist has to ensure to evidence for his/her conclusion/s.

7. Causes of a particular behaviour should never be mentioned.

8. Frame of reference must be clear while describing the child's performance. Like, instead of writing, "Her numerical aptitude is superior", it is better to write, "Her numerical aptitude is above the level of her other aptitudes".

9. Though the therapist collects lot of data through formal and informal methods but he/she should select whatever is relevant in relation to the presenting complaint. It is means that the therapist writes the report based on that data which is related to the purpose of the case study and to the related questions raised at the beginning.

10. The report is to be unique to the child with her high and low points in such a way that it cannot apply to other persons of same age, gender, or education in general.

11. Length of the report should nor compromise with its clarity.

The present chapter contains a few samples of reports written by different professionals. The purpose is to provide a clear guidance regarding the flow of a report. Names of clients have not been highlighted here but in reality, the names have to be written.

GOOD REPORT CONTAINS

1. Information about the assets and deficits of the client/child.
2. Content & language as per the reader.
3. Description of assessment devices.
4. Headings & lists for clarity of the communication.
5. Client/child is referred to by their name.
6. No writing about causes of a particular behaviour.
7. Brief report with use of technical terms when it is written for professionals.
8. Detailed report in simple language with explanation of technical terms used when written for parents and guardians.
9. Clarity & content of the report is of utmost importance.
10. Material or the content should not be repeated.
11. Sentences remain short with one concept presented in one sentence.
12. No more is written than necessary.

PITFALLS OF THE REPORT WRITING

i) Eisegesis: It is the problem of faulty interpretation based on personal ideas, bias, and what not. Quite often the psychologists use the same theories or draw the same conclusions in every report. The problem of eisegesis may also occur if the psychologist draws conclusions that are clearly in conflict with the data collected for a child.

ii) The length of the report should not compromise the accurate portrayal of the child's performance. The two main recipients of the report are teachers and parents who prefer clarity of the report above length. They generally prefer the report to answer their questions and address the distressing issues.

SAMPLE 1

Date: 28-07-08

Psychological Assessment Report

Name: - Miss V.S.	Education: - Class VII
Age: - 11 years 06 months	Informant: - Parents
Sex: - Female	Date of assessments: 09-04-2008, 04-07-08, & 11-7008.

Miss VS was brought by her parents for intellectual and scholastic assessment with complaints of poor academic performance.

Back-ground information: -
VS is an only child born after 14 years of marriage. She hails from an urban nuclear family and is studying in 7th class in Delhi Public School, Diamond Point, Secunderabad. There is no reported family history of Mental Illness, Mental Retardation or Epilepsy. Developmental history is also reported as normal. Assessment of the child was completed in three sessions.

Observation: -
Miss VS is a well-kept girl with an average built. She was well mannered and co-operative during the assessment. She could communicate fluently about herself and her interests similar to the children of her

age. Rapport could be established. Attention could be aroused and sustained for the required period. She was motivated for the testing and her comprehension of the test items was appropriate. Expressive speech was adequate for her age. Testing was completed in three sessions with adequate breaks in-between whenever required.

Tests administered: -
1. Malin's Intelligence scale for Indian children (MISIC)
2. Diagnostic Test of Learning Disability (DTLD)

Test findings: -
Miss VS was assessed with Malin's Intelligence scale for Indian Children (MISIC) and Diagnostic Test of Learning Disability (DTLD).

S.No.	Verbal Subtests		Performance Subtests	
1	Information	115	Picture completion	89
2	Comprehension	92	Block Design	107
3	Arithmetic	100	Object Assembly	81
4	Similarities	96	Coding	126
5	Vocabulary	102	Mazes	95
6	Digit Span (Not considered for Full scale IQ)	93		
	Verbal scale IQ	*102*	*Performance scale IQ*	*99.6*
	Full Scale IQ: 100			

On MISIC her verbal scale IQ was 102 and performance scale IQ was 99.6. Her **full-scale IQ** was calculated as **100** (Average IQ range 90-110) revealing an average level of intellectual functioning.

Her scores on subtests of MISIC are as follows:

She obtained her highest scores (115 in the Verbal scale subtest of Information, and on Performance scale subtest of coding (126).

The interpretation of the test results is suggestive of Miss VS having average abilities on verbal as well as performance domain subtests. **Diagnostic Test of Learning Disability** (DTLD) was administered on her to understand her pre-requisite abilities of learning. On DTLD, her scores in areas of Eye Hand Coordination, Figure Ground Perception, Figure Constancy, Cognitive Abilities, Spatial Relation, and Memory were found to be adequate.

Her scores on tests of Position in Space (5.5), Auditory Perception (4), Receptive Language (5), and Expressive Language (1.5) are inadequate. She obtained the lowest score in the subtest of Expressive language (1.5).

The test findings are suggestive of Miss VS having inadequate ability in the areas of expressive language and auditory perception. Though she has average intellectual functioning, she a specific inability in expressive abilities of language. This could be attributed for her poor performance in academics.

Impression:
From the information provided by parents, test results and observations, it can be derived that Miss VS is a child with learning difficulty in the areas of writing and reading. These could be partly influenced by inadequate exposure in writing and reading activities.

Name & Signature
(Rehabilitation Psychologist)

-x-

SAMPLE 2

ASSESSMENT REPORT

Registration No – 1148
Date of Registration- 30.12.2016

Miss V is a nine-year-old girl studying in class-IV. She was referred by school for a psychological evaluation to have an insight into her academic, social and emotional strengths. She was accompanied by her mother to the centre to seek guidance about her academic and behavioural issues.

Background Information of the Family

Miss V is the second child and belongs to a nuclear family. Her father is engaged in business and mother is working as a staff nurse in school. There is no family history of mental retardation, mental illness, convulsions and speech defect.

Physical Features
Physically the child was thinly built, neat and tidy. There was no physical deformity observed in her case, her fine and gross motor coordination and development was age appropriate. Her present height is 118 cm and weight is 23 kg.

Medical History
Ante natal History: Normal
Pre-natal History: A full term baby through normal delivery.
Neo-natal History: Child's neo natal condition was normal and all her milestones were in normal sequence.

School History
Child started her schooling at the age of two and a half years and was first admitted at Kidzee School in playgroup. Presently she is studying at C.M.S. since class – I.

Observation during Assessment
While observing and interacting with the Miss V, it was found that she was cooperative generally but seemed to be reserved. Though her communication skill was found to be age appropriate but she responded on verbal prompts on the part of observer. Her attention and concentration skills and understanding of general concepts was age appropriate.

Psychiatric Assessment: Revealed probability of Scholastic Backwardness with primary enuresis.

Name & Signature
(Social worker)

Note: The findings are based on one time testing as referred cases, not valid for medico legal purpose, to be correlated with clinical observation and history.

EDUCATIONAL ASSESSMENT

Test administered:
- Grade level Assessment Device for children with Learning Problems in School, by Dr. Jayanthi Narayan, NIMH, Secunderabad)
- Specific learning Disability, Comprehensive Learning Disability by Prof. Manju Mehta, Prof. Rajesh Sagar, AIIMS, New Delhi.

Test Results and findings:
- On GLAD, scored 50% on grade-II, and 30% on grade-III test in English an Hindi.

In mathematics, scored 30% on grade-II.
- On SLD(CDB), she performed on test item for 7-8 years of age.

Scores are as follows:
1. Reading- errors- 4 (Maximum possible errors- 3)
2. Writing- errors- 6(Maximum possible errors- 3)
3. Spelling English- 2/10 (Cut off score- 5)
4. Spelling Hindi- 3/10 (Cut off score-7)
5. Comprehension- error- 2(Maximum possible errors- 3)

Arithmetic

In addition- 3/4 (cut off score- 2)

Subtraction- 3/4 (cut off score- 2)

Multiplication- 3/4 (cut off score- 2)

Division- 2/4 (cut off score- 2)

Reasoning- 1/4

English reading and writing abilities/difficulties identified:
- Significantly below class level performance in both English and Hindi reading writing as compared to her current class level were noticed.

Mathematic Abilities/Difficulties identified.
- Computation skills- below average
- Mathematical reasoning and concepts- below average.

Impression:
Based on test results, behavioural observation, and detailed case history, the child is currently performing two grade lower than her current class level.

Recommendations:
- Parental counseling regarding child's abilities and difficulties in academic area and how can they help the child.

- Encouragement and support on the part of parents and teachers will increase child's self-confidence and self-esteem, thereby facilitate her learning process and overcome difficulties.
- Individual counseling of the child to enhance her self-confidence.
- Individualized education programme with to improve her academic skills in all subjects.
- Lot of oral reading exercises using phonetics on daily basis will improve his reading ability and speed.
- Use of reading material in big font size and colour cueing for the letters she confuses with.
- Identification of reading and writing errors can be done by doing error analysis and their correction would help in overcoming child's difficulty.

Name & Signature
(Special Educator)

-x-

SAMPLE 3

PSYCHOLOGICAL REPORT

Name: Mr. RR   Age: 24 years
Sex: male   Date of Testing: 12-06-2016

Chief complaints: The index person was accompanied by his father with the following chief complaints:

- Poor Memory.
- Low vision
- Head in injury at the age of 9 years
- Aggressive
- Poor scholastic performance
- Suicidal tendency

PERSONAL HISTORY:

Mother's age at conception was 25 years. Antenatal checkups were irregular. Birth cry was present. Birth weight was 1.7 kgs. Birth colour was pink. Post-natal history revealed immediate breast feeding; no other significant information was reported. Immunization was done as per schedule.

DEVELOPMENTAL HISTORY:

No developmental delay was reported.

FAMILY HISTORY:

RR is the third issue of a non-consanguineous marriage. It is a nuclear and intact family residing in rural locality. There is no history of MI or MR.

SCHOOL HISTORY:

He started schooling at the age of 5 in regular school in class one and studied till class ten. Poor academic performance was reported by the school.

OCCUPATION HISTORY:

He works in cybercafé as operator.

PROBLEM BEHAVIOUR:

Throws objects when angry.

TESTS ADMINISTERED:
  - ➤ DEVELOPMENTAL SCEENING TEST (DST)
  - ➤ VINELAND SOCIAL MATURITY SCALE (VSMS)
  - ➤ BINET-KAMAT INTELLENCE TEST (BKT)

BEHAVIORAL OBSERVATIONS:

RR looks age appropriate. He is well dressed, and maintains eye contact. Communicates verbally, and actively explores the environment. He gives sensible answers to questions. His attention could be aroused and sustained till the task was completed. He could comprehend 1-2 step instructions and was cooperative during assessment.

TEST RESULTS:

> On Developmental screening test (DST), he obtained Developmental age of 11 years, DQ was computed to be 73.
> On Vineland Social Maturity Scale (VSMS), he obtained a social age of 11 years 6 months; SQ was computed to be 77
> On BINET-KAMAT INTELLENCE TEST (BKT), he obtained a mental age of 10 years 6 months and computed IQ to be 66.

TEST INTERPRETATIONS:

> Test results of DST, VSMS and BKT reveal that RR is independent in self-help skills. Tells difference of objects, knows comparative values of currency, does small purchase and tells date and time. He distinguishes between friends and play mates.
> BKT test results indicate through his performance on language is of 14-years age norm, on memory sub-scale the scores indicate 10 years of age, and on non-meaningful memory it is 10 years, on conceptual thinking the scores reveal 9 years age norm, on non- verbal reasoning the client is indicating 12 years, and on verbal reasoning its 12 years of age level, numerical reasoning score indicate 14 years of age level, social intelligence score indicates 10 years of age.

DIAGNOSTIC IMPRESSION:

Based on the developmental history, personal history, behavioural observation, and results of tests administered, Mr. RR is currently functioning with Mild Intellectual Disability.

RECOMMENDATIONS:

> Parental counselling and guidance regarding the condition of the client.
> Life skill training

> ➢ Behaviour modification to reduce his problem behaviours.
> ➢ Regular follow ups.

Name & Signature
(PSYCHOLOGIST)

-x-

SAMPLE 4

Psychological Assessment Report

Name: - Master NC   Education: - LKG
Age: - 7 years, 11 months   Informant: - Parents
Sex: - Male   Date of assessment: 11/08/09

Master NC was brought to Research Centre for Special Needs Children by his parents for training and education.

Background Information: -
NC is an only child hailing from an urban joint family. There is no history of Mental Illness, Mental Retardation, or Epilepsy in the family as reported. He was born premature and underwent blood transfusion on 6th day after birth, and then he was diagnosed with Hydrocephalus and operated upon at the age of 6 months. Developmental milestones were delayed. Assessment was completed in one session.

Observations: -
NC is an average built, well-kept boy who understands Telugu very well. The assessment was done with the help of the in-charge of Special School Ms B. Instructions had to be repeated 4-5 times. Attention could be aroused and sustained for a few seconds. He was cooperative during the assessment. He is able to understand one-step instruction.

Test Administered: -
Binet Kamat Test of Intelligence (BKT).

Test Findings: -
Mental Age is coming to <u>4 years and 4 months.</u>
Chronological Age is 7 years and 11 months.

<u>**IQ** is **62.**</u>
From the information given by parents, observations, and test results master NC is having Mild Mental Retardation.

Name & Signature
(Rehabilitation Psychologist)

- The next chapter on Individualized Education Programme (IEP) is the most essential aspect in the education of children with exceptionality. It covers the historical background of IEP, it's components, role of Psychologists and behavioral approach, assessment for current level of functioning, goal setting, format for IEP and guidelines to fill part A and part B, lesson plan, and educational technology in India.

Dr Neerja Pandey

6

INDIVIDUALISED EDUCATION PROGRAMME (IEP)

HISTORICAL BACKGROUND

Individuals with disabilities were mostly neglected by the society and they were generally kept away from the mainstream society, at times in asylums for the rest of their lives. The trend and attitude of people started changing from 19th century onwards and since then the progress in the field of disability has been in leaps and bounds. This change happened in the education system also where children with disabilities were being encouraged to come to schools and study. Newer methods were developed to educate the disabled population in the way they can learn so that this population is not wasted, does not succumb to anti social elements for exploitation, become financially independent and finally become responsible citizens of the country. Their inner potential and resources can thus be profitably tapped with further training for which parents, teachers and professionals encouraged to actively get involved in the training and management of children with disabilities. One significant method that evolved is Individualized Education Programme/Plan (IEP). This term is sometimes inter changed with Individualised Training Programme (ITP).

Form and structure of the IEP, as is being discussed here, are an outcome of National seminar on development of IEP format held at National Institute for the Mentally Handicapped (NIMH) in 1986. Professionals like special educationists, speech pathologists and audiologists, psychologists, physio-occupational therapists and many more had participated in this seminar to discuss the existing IEP forms in the country and a new one was developed with the manual to fill it.

Feedback was provided after using the new format for 6 months based on which it was further modified. The IEP format and manual being successfully used by special schools in India are the revised one.

It is doubtless that each exceptional child is unique human being with her own range of intellectual and social assets and/or deficits. No two children with disability are the same even if they possess the same IQ or mental age. There will be differences between what they can do in comparison to the other. In this context, it is pertinent to ask if a common syllabus will benefit all the students with disability in our society. Obviously, we must have different teaching targets, methods, approaches, procedures, etc., for each child based on his or her current level of needs and performance. This is the essential objective of the IEP. It is an individualised training programme tailor-made to the needs of each disabled individual.

Each child with disability functions at a different level so it becomes necessary that the programme include the child's current level of functioning in different areas and what is expected of her from the environment she lives in.

ROLE OF PSYCHOLOGISTS

Psychologists are intricately involved with the team working with exceptional children. They do assessment, collect base-line data, plan the programme, and do the intervention.

- The assessment involves Diagnostic Assessment, Behavioural Assessment, Family Assessment, aptitude and interest assessment, and Prevocational and vocational assessment.
- Collection of base-line data includes Current level of cognitive functioning, Current level of social adaptive functioning, Current level of pre-vocational and vocational skills, Current level of educational and self-help skills

- Programme planning is about team work that involves professionals from multiple disciplines.
- Intervention is in areas of skill training, problem behaviour management and family intervention.

For the purpose of implementation of IEP, the psychologists assess skill behaviour and problem behaviour of the child concerned; record both skill as well as problem behaviours of the child as base-line recording; they use techniques to teach new behaviour and to cope up with problem behaviours; and evaluation continues through the intervention programme.

BEHAVIOURAL APPROACH TO IEP

Behaviour is a learnt activity that can be observed, measured, and recorded, and it has an objective. Both desirable and undesirable behaviours are learned and they can be unlearnt also. Everyone can learn a new behaviour as well as unlearn an older behaviour. For this purpose, reinforcers are used to teach and increase skill behaviours and techniques of punishment are used to decrease undesirable behaviour. This process is called Behaviour Modification (BM) Techniques which is very effective with exceptional children like children with autism, children with intellectual disabilities, children with conduct disorder and many other wide ranges of behavioral problems. In general also, BM techniques can be effectively used to teach certain desirable behaviours to small children.

Major COMPONENTS OF AN IEP
- General Background information about the child
- Current Level of Performance in specified skills
- Goals and short-term objectives
- Method and materials required to achieve the objective
- Evaluation to assess whether the objective is met

A well-planned IEP has information about a child's programme from many specialists like physiotherapist, occupational therapist, speech therapist, behaviour management, special educator and psychologist as and when these services are required. These services are coordinated by the special eductor.

Data is collected by taking detailed case-study of the child. It helps in understanding the child and the environment in which she is brought up. For example, if the child belongs to rural background, then the IEP would contain more of sketches and the teaching material would be from rural background. If the child has epilepsy, then the IEP would contain medical aspects as well.

ASSESSMENT

Assessment in IEP serves the purpose of guiding special educators in selection of goals and objectives because it includes information such as, what is the current level at which the child performs, learning style of the child (most effective sensory channel), problem behaviour that the child exhibits, and effective reinforcers. The teacher and special educators also need to differentiate between educationally relevant information and instructionally relevant information. Educationally relevant information is for placing the child in appropriate group and to plan the curriculum. Whereas, instructionally relevant information is needed to understand the child's strengths and weaknesses.

Now, the assessment is also divided into two criterions namely, norm-referenced tests and criterion-referenced tests. Standardized tests are norm-referenced criteria whereas teacher made tests are criterion-referenced assessment because they assess a child on a fixed criteria pre-decided by the teacher.

ASSESSMENT FOR CURRENT LEVEL OF FUNCTIONING

The teacher observes and makes note of the child for a specific behaviour. For example, a child sits and attends to an activity for about 2.5 or 3 minutes and then she starts running around, the teacher writes this behaviour as it is. She does not write it down as 'short attention span' or 'hyperactive' because this does not indicate what the child is currently able to do. When we write about a behaviour as it occurs then it is called writing in behavioral terms. Likewise, all areas of development including learning a skill and decrease of undesirable behaviour are all to be mentioned in behavioral terms, a skill that needs to be honed. Correct and precise assessment helps set appropriate goals, neither too high nor too low for the child. The assessment may take a week or more in the natural settings, and it is advised to take that time for the information to be precise.

The assessment of current level of functioning includes all the domains of development i.e., social development, emotional development, language development, along with time and money concepts, grade level functioning for scholastic levels etc.

GOAL SETTING

The IEP has two types of goals – annual goal and short-term goals. The annual goal is the anticipated achievement of a child in an academic year whereas shot-term-goals mean breaking the annual goal into small units or tasks. Appropriate need-based strategies are then applied to teach short-term tasks based on which the child would be taught the next level or unit. The short-term goals are based on sequential description of skills between where the child is now and where she is expected to be at the end of the last unit i.e. at the end of the academic year.

Teacher has to consider the child's pattern of progress or lack of lack of it from earlier trainings before developing an IEP. The goals should suit the child's ability. For example, for a child who is not yet toilet-trained, academics cannot be set as her goal. Thus, each child has different annual goals. Moreover, the goals are set from simple to complex with the condition that the child has prerequisite skills before learning the complex skills. Also, the goal set for home is different from the ones set for schools e.g. eating food independently is a goal to be achieved by parents whereas reading skill is to be taught by teacher. Therefore, the coordination between parents/caregivers and teachers is solicited.

The objectives of goals are set in behavioral terms with specific criteria for mastery, e.g. "When asked by the teacher, child will number five items in correct order, 8 out of 10 times by the end of three months". This behaviour is observable and measurable. After breaking the task to be taught into smaller units, they are put in a sequence. This process of breaking down the tasks into sequential components is called task analysis. The last short-term objective will be same as the annual goal in the particular skill. As long as each short-term goal follows the previous goal in logical and sequential order, it would be considered an appropriate strategy. The child should be given maximum opportunities to learn and experience.

EVALUATION

The child is evaluated regularly for further planning. In this process, unbiased evaluation on part of the teacher is of great value. Quantitative as well as qualitative analysis of the child's response help in realistic evaluation. Moreover, both verbal and written analysis give best results and parents are also involved in the development of IEP and training programme.

FORMAT FOR IEP

The IEP has two sections part A and part B. Part A consists of general information about the child, person initiating the programme, and the overall goals for the child. Part B consists of specific programming for a skill or behaviour.

GUIDELINES FOR FILLING UP PART A

1. Name: Child's full name and nickname (if any) in brackets
2. Date of birth (age): Given as in the records
3. Sex:
4. Address: Present address
5. Mother tongue/languages spoken: It is essential that the child is exposed to one language consistently. Therefore, record the details of the child's mother tongue as well as other language/s spoken by the child. Circle the mother tongue.
6. Registration Number: Give the number of the registration in the institute/school.
7. Class/Roll Number: In case of a special school, give the class group of the child and the roll number.
8. Date of writing the ITP: Indivudualised Training Propgramme (ITP) is generally written on a particular day when the team meets and decides on the programme for the child. Write the date of such a meeting.
9. ITP Number: The child will many ITPs following one after the other. Write the number of each ITP.
10. Significant information about the child: Includes details on: i. The degree of disability. ii. Associated conditions such as visual/ hearing or orthopedic handicap. Medical conditions such as epilepsy, hyperkinesia and behavioural problems. iii. Family background of the child. iv. Strengths and weaknesses of the child and v. Medicine taken (if any).
11. Goals: Mention the overall goals set for the child after assessment and the order of priority (If these are more than one goal)

12. Staff Responsible: The name of the staff member, whoever will be responsible for carrying out and coordinating the ITP should be mentioned here.

GUIDELINES FOR FILLING UP PART B

Part B consists of the specific programme for the child with precise instructions to carry out the programme.

13. Skill/Behaviour: Mention here, the skill on which the intellectually disabled child/individual is to be trained. For example, feeding skill, dressing skill or writing skill and so on. If it is a behaviour, which is to be modified, mention the name of the behaviour. For example, head banging, eye poking or body rocking, and so on.

14. Current level/Baseline: Write in behavioural terms what exactly the child is able to do in the given skill or behaviour. For example: If the skill is combing hair, the current level can be "picks up comb. Holds it appropriately. Places the comb on the head, but does not comb the hair in one direction uniformly. Cannot make the partition of the hair". If it is behaviour, mention what provokes the behaviour. The exact way in which the child behaves and for how long.

15. Objectives: Mention in behavioural terms what the objectives are to be. Mention the (a) Condition, (b) Behaviour, (c) Level of performance and (d) Deadline. To illustrate, an example is given below:

(a) When asked by the teacher to do so (b) the child (name of the child) will indicate to the appropriate picture of the fruit named (c) 8 out of 10 times correctly and (d) within 2 months' duration.

16. Procedure: Give step by step procedure for meeting the objective. Do not have ambiguous directions. The steps must be specific and clear. Remember to mention the reinforcers to be used and when.

17. Materials Needed: Write the materials needed for developing the particular skill or improving the particular behaviour.

18. Evaluation: Leave this column blank when the ITP is written after the specific duration when the child is evaluated for progress or problems. Fill this column by nothing down the observations. This, in turn, informs the baseline or current level of the next ITP to be written.

To quantify the progress of the child, performance may be ranked from 1 to 7 as shown below:

Below baseline = 1

No progress = 2

25% progress = 3

50% progress = 4

75% progress = 5

100% progress = 6

100% progress before deadline = 7

Circle the appropriate number. To get the percentage of progress, measure by comparing with the objective (8 out of 10 times). How many times the child is able to complete the task successfully. Find out the percentage of marks.

Skill development in speech and language, motor activities for daily living and academic areas can be written in this format as well as the problem behaviours to be corrected. Thus, the format is of use for special educators, speech pathologists, psychologists and the physiotherapists.

19. Problems Encountered/Remarks:

Write here clearly, the problems faced while carrying out the programme which maybe specific to the child and the situation.

INDIVIDUALISED TRAINING PROGRAMME

9.1 PART-A

1	Name		Registration No.	
	Date of birth (Age)		Class and Roll No.	
	Sex		Date of Filling ITP	
	Address			
2	Mother Tongue/ Languages spoken by the child			
3	Significant Information about the child			
4	Associated Conditions (If Any)			
5	Referral to other services			

6	Annual Goals	

PART-B

ITP No.	
Date of Programming	
Date of Evaluation	
Persons Responsible	

1	Area/Domain	
2	Task / Skill / Activity	
3	Present Functioning Level / Current Functioning Level / Baseline	

4	Specific Objectives / Instructional Objectives	
5	Materials Needed	
6	Procedure	

Dr Neerja Pandey

7	Reinforcement	
8	Evaluation	

10. TASK ANALYSIS RECORD

Task: **Name of the child:**

                                            Age/Sex:

Criteria: **Class:**

Sub Tasks	Date											
	Session											
Number of Success: **Percentage:**												

Key: + = Yes, **C** = Occasional Cues, **VP** = Verbal Prompt, **GP** = Gestural Prompt, **MP** = Modelling Prompt, **PP** = Physical Prompt

Dr Neerja Pandey

INSTRUCTIONAL STRATEGIES

One teacher to one student is often recommended in individualized instruction set up but it can be achieved with one teacher to a group of students as well.

GROUP INSTRUCTIONS

Two methods are used to teach group of students - sequential instructions and concurrent instructions. In sequential instruction, the teacher goes from one student to another to teach each student individually. Students in the group may learn either same skills or different skills. Alternatively, the teacher may choose to give general instructions or demonstrations (at the same time) to the group before beginning to give sequential instructions.

For concurrent instructions, following points are to be kept in mind:
   a)   Students in the group must be at similar level of achievement.
   b)   They should be able to learn from the same methods of teaching.
   c)   They must have relatively well-developed language skills (verbal or manual).
   d)   They must be able to imitate a teacher's demonstration/s.

Depending upon the group and ability of the students, the teacher can practice either sequential instruction or concurrent instruction.

LESSON PLAN

The teacher prepares the lesson plan to use it as a blue print and guide in effective teaching. It also helps in completing a task within the time-frame. It can be prepared as per either sequential instruction or concurrent instruction. The teacher can plan individualized instruction, small group instruction, or large group instruction for her class. For example, if it is a math class and the teacher intends to teach counting objects then she has to consider the current level of children in the group:
   •   One child may not have counting ability at all
   •   One child may be able to count up to 2
   •   One child may be able to count up to 5

If the teacher starts teaching number-values and if she is not prepared the lesson plan then she will have difficulty taking care of difficulty level of each child or she may teach same concept to all children who in turn won't be able to grasp the concept.

The lesson plan helps the teacher in following manner:
  (a) What will she be teaching?
  (b) What will be the classroom arrangement?
  (c) How will she be starting the lesson?
  (d) What materials and methods she would be using?
  (e) How would she be teaching?
  (f) What reinforcers would she be using?
  (g) How will she evaluate the lesson?
  (h) How will she conclude the lesson?

INSTRUCTIONAL MATERIALS

Instructional materials are required for teaching skills to children with disabilities. Different types of material like, concrete objects, models, pictures, flash cards, audiovisuals, puppets charts, software packages, play material, etc. are all used by teachers in classrooms during teaching. It has been noted in literature that teaching materials and aids promote multi-sensory learning. As students use/manipulate the material by themselves, it creates an interactive environment between the teacher and the students. In addition, students need a novel experience that may sustain their interest. Therefore, a teacher has to plan a variety of activities using material to make the teaching learning environment more conducive for learning.

LEARNING AIDS AND FUNCTIONAL AIDS

As education of children with disabilities aims at preparing them to be independent as far as possible, it becomes essential to identify certain aids which facilitate independent functioning in the community. For example, while teaching the names of vegetables, the teacher may use the concrete vegetables, models, flash cards, charts (learning aids), for teaching the content. However, for a student who is non-verbal and has to go to a vegetable shop to buy vegetables, the teacher may provide a pocket picture album to remember or to ask the shopkeeper. The picture album (functional aid) can have many more pictures for facilitating communication for the student. The function of the learning aid ceases once the student learns the concept whereas the need for functional aid continues as the student requires it for independent living.

GUIDELINES FOR USING LEARNING AIDS

It is apparent that the material which interests one child may not interest another child. Hence, a teacher has to be always observant, and vigilant to notice such individual differences among children and should select and/or develop the teaching learning materials to make learning effective for each child.

Following are some general guidelines to be followed:
- Use of concrete material as far as possible in the initial stages (acquisition stage) of teaching the concepts.
- Selection of pictures/flash cards that look like real or near real objects.
- Use of age-appropriate teaching learning material.
- Appropriateness of the teaching aid or material to the topic being taught.
- The material selected or developed should be such that it can be used for teaching many concepts.
- Selection of a variety of materials and plan a number of activities to provide novelty.
- Presentation of the material in such a way that all students can have a clear view of the material.

EDUCATIONAL TECHNOLOGY

Advancements in technology have made it possible to innovate electronic devices that supplement and/or support persons with disabilities in learning and leading their lives meaningfully and fruitfully. To name some, electronically operated wheel chairs, walking aids, hearing aids, adaptations in computer peripherals, educational software are found to be of immense help to the needy persons.

Apart from the electronic technology, the information technology (IT) has brought a revolution in their life and lifestyles. The information, which was accessible to only a few people before, is accessible today to almost everyone through easily accessible internet web sites. Professionals, family members and others are able to compile information on new developments, trends and innovations in teaching process of children with disabilities thorugh surfing relevant web sites. This helps them in updating the knowledge to keep pace with the changes and advancements taking place in the field of special education. Further, the inventions, both in electronic and information technology have paved way to distance mode of education. With this, a large number of persons in remote and inaccessible areas can avail educational facilities.

USE OF EDUCATIONAL TECHNOLOGY

Technology is the application of scientific knowledge to the practical tasks of life. If properly developed, technology could make education more productive, individualized and powerful for learning recent information, make instructions more scientifically based and provide access to education for all.

Educational technology is defined as a complex, integrated process involving people, procedure, ideas, device and organizations for analyzing problems and devising, implementing, evaluating and managing solutions to these problems involved in all aspects of learning. (Thomas, 1987). One of the purposes of educational technology is to promote the efficacy of education. Educational technology is used for:

- Effective instruction
- Facilitating individual differences
- Providing equal educational opportunities
- Preservation of knowledge
- Imparting quality education
- Educational planning
- Pre-service and in-service teacher education, and
- Find solutions for problems in Indian educational systems

EDUCATIONAL TECHNOLOGY IN INDIA

Technology includes a) Hardware device or media, b) Software or programmed instruction, c) Planning, designing and analyzing programmes.

The growth and development of educational technology is based on the new innovations and advancements in technology. For example, visual instructions (pictures, slides, audio, video films) were largely developed with the invention of photography, radio, tape recorder, television, slide projector and overhead projector. The recent developments in educational technology is the transmission of audio and televised instruction and/or information by communication satellites. In addition, the invention of information technology made it possible to have an access to information in all spheres of life.

In 1973, units were established at National Council of Educational Research and Training (NCERT) and in the Department of Education at Delhi to develop education technology. In addition, educational technology cells were established in different states of India and the four Regional Colleges of Education at Bhopal, Ajmer, Mysore and Bhubaneswar. Agencies such as University Grants Commission (UGC) and Indira Gandhi National Open University (IGNOU) are engaged in the creation and use of educational technology in general, and educational media in particular and the programmes are transmitted through various communication media. *Doordarshan* (National Television) and All India Radio are also being used to telecast the educational programmes effectively. In addition, internet is the world's largest computer networking system which serves as an information provider, publisher and instructor. It is the cheapest and fastest means of access to information.

SUMMARY

a) Education of children with disabilities involves assessment of current level of functioning of students, planning an individualized education programme (IEP), implementation of planned programme, evaluation and recording of the performance/achievement of students, and informing the progress to parents/family members. Important features of programme planning is that the parents/family members take up a partnership role in IEP meetings in deciding the content to be taught to the students.

b) The contents of the IEP include documentation of students present/current level performance, indication of specific services and type of programme to be provided, annual goals, short-term objectives, and procedures and schedules for evaluating goals and objectives.

c) Individualized instruction, small groups and large group instruction are commonly practiced in special schools by the teachers.

d) Sequential instruction and or concurrent instruction are used while teaching groups of students as per the individual requirement and based on the homogeneity of the group.

e) Appropriate teaching learning materials and functional aids are selected and developed for the purpose of teaching various concepts and for functioning independently in the community.

f) Electronic technology and information technology have brought a revolution in the life and life styles of persons with disabilities.

g) Educational software packages are developed all over the world and also in India for teaching academic skills to children with intellectual disabilities.

- The next chapter is on Behaviour Modification Techniques (BM) because it is one of the widely used techniques that works effectively with children. It explains behaviour and behaviour modification, historical background of BM, Premise of BM that covers problem behaviours, skill behaviours, steps to be followed in BM, techniques of decreasing problem behaviour and techniques of increasing skill behaviours, reinforcers and methods of selecting reinforcers, method of group rewards, and two samples case study in BM.

7

BEHAVIOUR MODIFICATION TECHNIQUES

One of the techniques that works best with children is Behaviour Modification Technique or simply put BM. It is very effective with exceptional children like Children with autism, children with intellectual disabilities, children with conduct disorder and many other wide ranges of behavioral problems. In general also, BM techniques can be effectively used to teach certain desirable behaviours to small children. For the purpose of behaviour modification we need to understand what behaviour is, which behaviour needs to be modified and why because, every behaviour is not supposed to be changed or modified. There are certain guidelines according to which we select an undesirable behaviour that has to be changed. And then there are certain techniques, based on learning principles, which are used to modify a particular behaviour. At the same time, we enhance and teach certain skills to the child to counteract the undesirable behaviour. The techniques used are: identification and definition of target behaviour, functional analysis of the behaviour, selection of reinforcers and punishment, training programme, and continuous assessment.

Behaviour

Behaviour, in reference to behaviour modification, is that activity which can be observed, measured and recorded and which has an objective. The premise is that every behaviour is a learnt behaviour and because it has been learnt so it can be unlearnt also. Learning and unlearning follow the same principles of learning. Some behaviours are maintained because there is a payoff, it serves a purpose i.e. the child is getting some benefit by continuously behaving in the same manner. Both, the skill behaviour as well as the deficit behaviour (lack of skill behaviour) are learnt behaviours. For example, a child gets a pat on her head every time she points to a banana and says the word 'banana'. On the other hand, another child learns to shout and cry because every time she shouts the teacher gives her a toy to play with and she likes to get the toy. Now the teacher does not give any toy to the child who cries and shouts. Instead the teacher ignores her when she cries and shouts. Initially, the shouting and crying will increase in intensity but with teacher's consistency of ignoring behaviour, the child learns to stay quiet in order to get the toys. Thus, she has unlearnt the problem behaviour. Sometimes, good behaviours are learnt to avoid unpleasant consequences like wearing sweater to avoid cold, carry umbrella to avoid rain, study to avoid punishment etc.

Behaviour Modification (BM)

The term Behaviour Modification was coined by practitioners to highlight behavioral deficits and excesses of behaviour at times. The goal is to reinforce desirable behaviors and eliminate the undesirable ones. BM is rooted in the principles of behaviorism, a school of thought focused on the idea that we learn from our environment. Its application has been picked up from experimental research done with laboratory animals. The focus of treatment is on current problems and how to change them. BM is an educational endeavor and it refers to outcome rather than the method. So, it does not distinguish between various means of changing behaviour. Behaviour Modification can simply be defined as 'use of learning theory principles to teach adaptive behaviour or alter maladaptive behaviour' or 'the process or methods which are to increase desirable behaviours and decrease undesirable problematic behaviour'. A behaviour can be maladaptive or deficient. Deficient behaviour is that behaviour which a child has failed to learn whereas maladaptive behaviour is that behaviour where a child has learnt inappropriate response/s.

When learning principles are used systematically to teach or alter a specific predetermined behaviour then the label 'Behaviour Modification' is aptly applied. Parents and caregivers are also taught the technique so that they can use the same at home.

Historical Overview

The major contributors in the field of BM are Ivan P. Pavlov, Edward L. Thorndike, John B. Watson and B.F. Skinner. Pavlov worked on conditioned reflexes, Thorndike's contribution is law of effect, Watson started the Behavioristic movement and Skinner expanded the field of behaviorism. Skinner's work on operant conditioning became the foundation of Behaviour Modification. Some psychologists trace the birth of BM to two experiments – 'Little Albert experiment' by Watson and 'Peter's fear of rabbits' by Mary Cover. Many researches have been conducted to demonstrate behavioral principles that highlight the research conducted on adult behaviour, children's behaviour, and on individuals with mental illness. It successfully has been used in prisons as well. Plenty of books and journals have also come up that showcase the work done in the field of Behaviour Modification.

Premise of BM

All behaviours can be divided into two categories – Skill Behaviours and Problem Behaviours.

Skill Behaviours
Skill behaviours can also be referred to as desirable behaviour (because it is desired that the child learns it) or deficit behaviour (because it is lacking in the child). The skill or deficit target behaviour is increased in its intensity, frequency and duration. For convenience and easy

understanding the skill behaviours can be classified into following domains:

- Motor skills like jumping, skipping, running, walking, unscrewing a bottle cap, pouring water from one container to another without spilling.
- Activities of daily living like drinking water from glass, eating with own hands without dirtying the clothes, brushing teeth, self-bathing with all the sub activities involved, undressing and dressing the self, self-grooming like combing the hair etc. Toileting like understanding and indicating the toilet needs, washing self after toilet use etc.
- Language skills including both receptive as well as expressive language.
- Reading and writing skills.
- Number and time concepts.
- Domestic and social activities like drying the clothes, greeting people appropriately, helping in household chores and taking on certain responsibilities.
- Basic money concepts.

Problem Behaviours

Problem behaviours may also be referred to as undesirable behaviour or behavioural excess (because certain behaviour is done in excess making rendering it undesirable). Many a times children exhibit behaviour that is considered problematic and put strain on teachers and parents alike. Efforts are made to decrease their frequency, duration and intensity. These are put into following broad categories:

- Violent and destructive behaviour like tearing books, breaking things, throwing objects, hitting others etc.
- Damage property like tears/pulls threads from clothing, damages furniture etc.
- Dangerous to other people.
- Temper tantrums like crying incessantly, rolling on the floor, screaming etc.

- Misbehaviour with others like snatching things, spitting on others, using abusive language etc.
- Self-injurious behaviours like banging the head on the wall, pulling own hair, biting the self, peeling the skin from wounds, picking at wounds on own body etc.
- Repetitive behaviour like rocking the body, nodding head, shaking a part of the body repeatedly etc.
- Odd behaviours like smiling, laughing, talking to self without reason etc.
- Hyperactivity like not sitting at one place for required time, not completing the task at hand etc.
- Rebellious behaviour like refusing to obey the instructions, doing opposite of what is requested etc.
- Antisocial behaviour like stealing, lying, cheating in games, twisting the truths, blaming others etc.
- Fear of places, people, objects or animals.

Causes of Problem Behaviour

No one single cause is known that causes behaviour problem. There are several factors that may contribute towards development of behavioral issues such as biological factors, social factors, cognitive or emotional factors. Generally, these factors are interwoven and are identified by the parents first and later, through behaviour checklist/s.

Steps to be followed in BM

There are five major steps in implementing Behaviour Modification Techniques or Programme:

1. Identification of the problem behaviour and behavioral assessment with help of parents' report, teachers' report, interview (of parents, teachers and caregivers), direct observation of the child and behavioral checklist or rating scales. In fact,

combination of all these techniques yield best result. The assessment should ideally be done at three occasions namely, before starting the training programme (it is called baseline assessment), during the assessment at three months (it is called quarterly assessment) and at the end of the training programme (it is called programme evaluation). Behavioral assessment is to acquire information about the, a) current level of skill behaviour in the child and b) current level of problem behaviour in the child.

Behavioral assessment helps us to know the a) The specific skill behaviours present in the child b) The specific skill behaviours not present in the child c) The specific skill behaviours to be targeted for training d) The types of problem behaviour present in the child e) The specific problem behaviour to be targeted for management f) Whether the behaviour modification is effective for a given child or not?

Defining target behaviours: Identified behaviour is defined in observable, objective, clear and measurable terms. For example, note the behaviour in terms of what the child actually does or does not. Secondly, hierarchy of problems to be made based on severity. And finally, Selection of one or two behaviours from the list that need to be changed. This identified behaviour is now called the target behaviour.

2. Behaviour recording (baseline and treatment). Record of the behaviour is maintained to monitor target behaviour as well as to evaluate the effectiveness of ongoing therapy.
3. Functional/Behavioral Analysis of the target behaviour follows the A-B-C model i.e. record of antecedent condition (event happening just before the occurrence of undesirable behaviour), the behaviour itself, and consequences of that behaviour. Functional analysis helps in identification of relationship between the environment and a particular behaviour. It helps

in understanding why the behaviour is being maintained. Identification of rewards is also done at this stage.

4. Development and implementation of Behaviour Training Programme (BMP), its procedures and their continuous evaluation. Parents and caregivers are also involved the training programmes because they have to follow the same procedures at home.

GUIDELINES FOR DEVELOPMENT OF BEHAVIOUR TRAINING PROGRAMME (BMP)

I) Techniques for decreasing undesirable behaviours

These techniques, generally, are used in different combinations. Appropriate techniques have to be selected depending upon individual problem and the functional analysis.

1. Restructuring the environment/modification of the environment: No behaviour takes place in a vacuum. It is dependent upon certain situations either in the present environment or in the immediate past and that event is called 'stimuli'. So, if it is clear in functional analysis that the undesirable behaviour occurs in one environmental setting and not in other then that environmental setting is restructured or modified. For example, a child is distracted because of his peers then a screen can be put between her and her peers, sitting arrangement can be changed, or isolate her. Thus, distracting stimuli is reduced in the classroom. But it has to be used in combination with positive reinforcement i.e. reinforcement is used when the child does her task, and withhold the reinforcement if the undesirable behaviour re-occurs in new environment.

   Environment may be described in terms of its physical properties like a city park (with its grass, trees and play equipment) or in terms of its functional properties (like one child loves to go this city park because of happy association and another child may not like to go this park due to negative and unhappy associations like getting injured and going to hospital.

This is a technique where emphasis is more on prevention of problem behaviour. The restructuring can be done by changing the antecedent factors like particular place, situation, presence of a person, specific demands placed on the child, appropriateness of the task, methods of instruction used by parents. One has to identify what are those factors that lead to a particular Problem Behaviour, then the antecedent factors can be avoided / changed to manage the problem behaviour. Sometimes it may not be possible to control the antecedents in the natural environment, the other techniques of controlling the consequence factors can be used for effective management of problem behaviour.

2. Extinction: The discontinuation or withholding of the reinforcer that has previously been reinforcing it is called extinction. This process is also known as Systematic Ignoring. Frequency of a behaviour is reduced by not giving the reinforcer. It is progressive weakening of a behaviour through repeated non-reinforcement. For example, a child has tantrums by loud screaming whenever she is asked to read. The teacher stops the task of reading. Functional analysis revealed that loud screaming was being reinforced/encouraged by the teacher by not letting the child read. The extinction programme here involves not giving the reinforcement and continue the task of reading despite the tantrum. It is effective only when the teacher / parent is consistent in implementation of the intervention guidelines.

It cannot be used for behaviours that are self-injurious or injurious to others or when the target behaviour exhibited remains impassive or when no verbal sermons have been given. Extinction bursts seen immediately after initial implementation.

3. Punishment: Introduction of consequences that reduce the chances/probability of occurrence of undesirable behaviour in future. The punishing consequences/stimulus for a particular child can be elicited through functional analysis. During the analysis itself it has to be ascertained as to what stimulus will act as reinforcer and what as punishment. Punishment procedure should be used immediately and consistently following the undesirable behaviour for it to be effective. Following are the common types of punishment procedures.

4. Time out: It is the removal of a child from an apparently reinforcing setting to a presumably non-reinforcing setting for a specified and limited period of time. It is a procedure in which the child is placed in a different less-rewarding situation or setting whenever she engages in undesirable or inappropriate behaviour but it is to be used in tandem with other discipline techniques. Time out is only for a short duration till the child stops the undesirable behaviour. For example, time out may be used when a student confronts with teaching staff at the same time a reinforcement/reward may be used when the same student complies courteously to teacher request. Assessment and record of time out is to be done so that the child is not using time out as an escape from the task assigned to her because then time out would encourage the escapist behaviour. In such case it is to be stopped immediately because time out is intended to reduce the frequency of the target behaviour. It has two types Exclusion and Isolation and moreover, it is not to be used for self-stimulatory behaviours. If the child indulges in desirable behaviour after coming from time-out, then she deserves reward.

   - Response cost: It is the cost which an individual pays for the response he makes. The child loses the benefits she used to get earlier because she had earned it for good behaviours and for not indulging in undesirable behaviour. This procedure is used in those-setup where token economy is being used to teach a skill or increase a desirable behaviour. When undesirable behaviour occurs then a fixed number of tokens, stars or points are deduced from what the child has already earned. It can be used as punishment for abusive language, aggressive behaviour, or for late coming. One very important condition is that the Child must have the cognitive ability to make a link between gaining & losing.

- <u>Over correction</u> involves two procedures, a) restituition and b) positive practice. Restitution means restoration of something lost or disturbed and positive practices involves practicing appropriate mode of response in the same situation in which the child was misbehaving. For example, if the child keeps eating rubbish found on the ground (a condition called pica), restitutional over-correction would involve prolonged period (say 15 minutes) of teeth, mouth, and hand washing with soap or antiseptic every time the behaviour occurs. Positive practice would involve (after the restitution of 15 minutes) appropriate ways of handling the rubbish like sweeping the floor, mopping and throwing away the garbage in dust bin etc.

- <u>Restraint</u>. Physical restraint is effective in reducing self-injurious physical aggressive behaviours and the likes. Restraint varies depending upon the child. It could be restraining the child on a chair or holding the child's hands lightly on the sides for a short duration, holding the child's head tightly between the palms of the trainer, keeping the child's head between the knees, etc. Emphatic 'No' proceeds the restraint.

- <u>Restoring the damage</u>: Let the student restore the damage done e.g. if he/she has thrown paper in the class then ask him/her to pick that paper.

- <u>Conveying displeasure/pleasure</u>: Verbally convey the displeasure and convey exactly what behaviour was undesirable & do it immediately. Explain the expected behaviour while conveying displeasure. Similarly, convey pleasure when the child behaves appropriately. It means, praise and/or criticize the behaviour of the child, NOT the child.

- Aversion: This method is used only when all other training methods have failed to control the undesirable behaviour. Life threatening or self-injurious behaviour like severe head banging, or persistent vomiting and biting are controlled by aversive stimuli. Battery operated mild shock (faradic aversion) is administered immediately following the undesirable behaviour.

5. Differential reinforcement is defined as the process of reinforcing an appropriate behaviour in the presence of one stimulus and simultaneously not reinforcing a behaviour in the presence of another stimulus. This programme involves positive reinforcement for occurrence of desirable behaviour specified in advance, absence of undesirable behaviour for a specific period of time, and occurrence of behaviour which is incompatible with target behaviour to be reduced. Differential reinforcement should always be added when a punishment is being used to reduce an undesirable behaviour. Otherwise problem behaviour tends to get maintained because of lack of adaptive/skill behaviour. It means that problem behaviour has to be replaced by skill behaviour.

II) Techniques for increasing desirable behaviours

Behaviour is determined by its consequences. The behaviour is continued if the consequences are pleasant. Parents and teachers make children learn by encouragement, praise and rewards. This is known as reinforcement or simply reward. Reinforcement is any event that is followed by a behaviour which strengthens the probability or frequency of occurrence of that behaviour. Reinforcer does not always mean 'pleasant' or 'something nice'. It is any event that increases the probability of a behaviour.

Some Reinforcers:

1. Primary reinforcer: These are essential for life i.e. reinforcers like eatables, food items, drink, sleep etc.

2. Material rewards: things or articles liked by the child like ball, kite, marbles, particular toys etc.

3. Activity: Actions and behaviours liked to be performed by the child like sketching, skipping the rope, dancing, listening to music, playing with pets, riding cycle etc.

4. Privileges: Privileges are special status/positions that the child likes to occupy. The procedure involves placing the child in that status or position which will make her feel important like becoming class monitor or line monitor, leader of the group, or getting a responsibility by the teacher etc.

5. Secondary reinforcer: Events and objects that have property of reinforcers because of pairing with primary reinforcer like money or points etc.

6. Social reinforcer: These are events that have significance at emotional level and it can be verbal as well as non-verbal like attention, praise (good, nice, keep it up, shabaash so on and so forth), hugging, pat, kiss, nod, getting a star or good in the notebook etc.

7. Token economy: Tokens are items that do not have value but gain meaningful value by getting associated with other items. The child receives a token (like golden or silver star, coins, or tick-mark in notebooks) immediately after displaying a desirable behaviour. Tokens are collected and later exchanged for meaningful objects or privileges by the child. Teachers can devise any item with token value so that children will like them and begin to work for them.

8. Shaping: Knowing 'how to reinforce' is a major aspect in behaviour modification. In shaping, the behaviour is reinforced step-by-step. The therapist starts by reinforcing the existing behaviour. Once it is established, he reinforces the response that is closest to the desired behaviour and ignores the other responses. For example, to establish eye to eye contact, the

therapist will sit opposite the child and reinforce her even if she moves her upper body towards the therapist. Once this is established then he will reinforce the head movement in his direction. And this procedure continues till eye-to-eye contact is established.

9. Prompting: The therapist initially, physically guides the child to look at him by turning her head towards him and this is reinforced. Prompting is effectively used in teaching self-help skills.

10. Cueing: While the therapist physically guides the child to look at him, he takes the child's name and says 'Look at me'. This serves as a cue to the child. Later by just telling her to look at the therapist, she looks up. Gestural cues, verbal cues and prompting are effectively used in language training.

11. Fading: Fading is always used with prompting and cueing. Once the child learns to do something then the therapist fades out the prompting and cuing.

12. Chaining: It is used when a child fails to perform a complex task. The complex task is broken into a number of small steps and each step is taught to the child. This is the basis of chaining technique. The child is trained to master a chain of behaviours. Chaining technique is particularly used in teaching self-help skills. In forward chaining, one starts with the first step, goes on to the second step, and to the third and so on. In backward chaining, one starts with the last step and goes on to the next step in backward fashion. Backward chaining is found to be more effective in training of mentally challenged children.

13. Imitation/Modeling: Children imitate the behaviour of their parents and teachers. In this method, the existing behaviour is modified by observing other people's behaviour. Prompting is needed with imitation. In imitation, the model also gets reinforcement for the correct response to indicate to the child that reinforcement occurs after the correct response. Peer models are found to be better imitated than models. Some children

Dr Neerja Pandey

prefer to imitate adults. So, the choice of model depends on the child.

14. Generalization: If a behaviour taught in a particular place is exhibited in another place also then it is said that generalization has taken place. In exceptional children, generalization is a slow process and appearance of a particular desired behaviour may be situation specific. So, efforts to generalize the skills learnt is part of behaviour modification programme.

15. Discrimination: The child is taught the specific environmental conditions in which a particular behaviour is appropriate. Technique of differential reinforcement is used to achieve the ability to discriminate. Only the correct responses in a particular situation are reinforces and incorrect responses are punished.

III) Methods of selecting appropriate reinforcers

- Ask the child directly.
- Ask the parents, siblings, or the caretakers.
- Offer a variety of reinforcers like food items and drinks to the child and see what she chooses most often.
- In children who have no particular preferences, observe the child and see what she does most often. Then use this preference as reinforcement say for example, wandering off from the seat. So, wandering away is allowed after completing the task.
- Choose rewards that are easily available and dispensable and that are not very expensive.
- Choose appropriate rewards i.e. appropriate for age, sex, and other individual needs of the child.
- Choose a reward strong enough to elicit the desired behaviour in the child.
- Change the rewards frequently as the children get bored easily with same items. They need novelty. Moreover, children undergo changes and their preferences also change.

Reward or reinforcement is something that happens after a behaviour has occurred & makes that behaviour to occur again in future. It is something that a child likes or feels good about and it may not always be something that the teacher or the parent thinks the child should like.

IV) Presentation of Reinforcers

- Contingency: Reward to be given only when the desired behaviour occurs.
- Consistency: Behaviour should be reinforced every time it occurs especially during the initial stages of the training programme.
- Clarity: The child should be clearly aware that the reinforcement has been given for a purpose.
- Immediacy: Reinforcement should be given soon after the desired behaviour occurs. "*A reward delayed is equal to reward denied.*"
- Giving reward in step-by-step fashion starting from the level child is able to perform e.g. if the child is able to scribble then reward the circular scribbling, then for single circle shapes going on to proper circles.
- Reward the specific behaviour rather than the child i.e. "Good, I liked the way you correctly answered the question." Do not say - "Good boy."
- Giving active assistance i.e.
  a) physical prompting
  b) verbal prompting
  c) clueing
- Process of gradual decrease in active assistance from teacher toward independent performance by the student.
- Combination: Combine social rewards/reinforcers along with other rewards. Like primary rewards to be used simultaneously with social rewards so that as the child begins to work for social rewards then primary rewards can be gradually reduced and finally withdrawn.
- Tone & facial expression should convey happiness.

- Appropriate amount: Use of either too little or too much reinforcement may not be effective. Identify and use right quantity of reward that is effective for each child.
- Fading: As the child acquires the behaviour rewards need to be faded. Rewards are removed gradually so that they can be re-introduced for learning of other new behaviours.

V)   Group Reward Techniques

Following procedures can be used to specify the rules for getting rewards in classroom or group settings:

- Specify the rules in pictorial and written form on the notice board in the classroom.
- State the rules of getting the reward at the beginning of each period in clear and understandable terms in front of all the children in the class or group.
- To make sure children have understood, ask any one child to tell the rules of getting reward in their own words. If the child knows that occurrence of a specific target behaviour will fetch her a reward then she would work for it.
- Draw the attention of other children towards the child who receives a reward. Make sure that other children understand for what behaviour this child is getting the reward.
- Important: *No undue comparisons or adverse remarks be made about students not receiving rewards*.

Purpose of Giving Rewards

- Rewarding clearly will help the child understand why he/she has been rewarded.
- It helps the child to learn the relationship between specific behaviour & reward received.
- Child understands that you accept or reject the behaviour & not the child.
- Always use positive statements about the child e.g. "child is able to do this much."

- Instead of focusing on & correcting the faults, we need to look at desirable deeds of a child. Attend to the strengths & assets of the child and encourage them.

Guidelines for Effective Teaching
- Easy to difficult
- Familiar to unfamiliar
- Concrete to abstract
- Whole to part

Factors in high-quality child care
- Caregiver's / teachers' educational preparation.
- Caregiver's / teachers' personal commitment to learning about and taking care of the children.

Appropriate Way of Giving Instructions
- No choice in the instruction like "Will you do it or not?"
- It should be to the point in clear wordings.
- One instruction at a time.
- Make sure you have the attention before giving out any instruction.
- Make the child repeat the instruction.
- Allow for reaction time.

Positive Behaviour Support (PBS)

The approach used for giving individualised intervention called Positive Behavior Support (PBS) is a new concept that was researched extensively during 1980s. it incorporates applied behaviour analysis, concept of inclusive education, and person-cantered aspects within its purview. The comprehensive approach was introduced by Koegel and his associates in 1996. They emphasised to alter the environment before problem behaviour arises and also on teaching appropriate behaviour so as to reduce the problem behaviour. It highlights the movement towards personal competence in social sciences and education.

Formats for BM is attached in the appendix.

Summary

We have a child who has certain problem behaviours. Using behaviour check-list we make a list of behaviours in the order of severity taking help from parents and teachers. We pick up the most severe problem behaviour as the target behaviour and analyse it to see if it is problem behaviour or is it deficit behaviour. If it is a problem behaviour then which behaviour will replace that problem behaviour. We decide upon strong reinforcers and punishments to be used. We prepare the schedule and start the training programme.

- The next chapter on Rehabilitation is covering the difference between habitation and rehabilitation, need and history of rehabilitation, importance of rehabilitation services, models of rehabilitation, assessment and parental role.

8

CASE STUDIES OF BEHAVIOUR MODIFICATION TECHNIQUES (BM)

SAMPLE 1

Master SS

Sex: Male   **DOB**:11 /0/1997

Age: 7 years 8 months   **Father's name**: Mr. M

Mother's name: Mrs. MB   **Follow up**: May 2006

Date of Assessment: 17/05/2006

Master SS had reported with his mother on 25th April 2006 with complaints of scholastic backwardness, diurnal enuresis and epilepsy/ fits. The first attack of epilepsy had been at 1 year of age and the last attack had been at 8 years of age on 21st April 2006. (The following sample of Behaviour Modification report is from sessions taken after the Case Study intake.)

History: Master SS is third child born to a couple who are in consanguineous marriage and who live in joint family. His father is Hearing Handicapped and his elder sister had fits till age 5. Master SS has a history of delayed birth cry and delayed speech. He spoke his first word at 5 years of age. He is on medication for fits as well as for involuntary passing of urine even during waking hours. He goes to regular school but his academic performance is poor. Sometimes SS helps his mother at home.

Developmental Screening Test (DST)	Vineland Social Maturity Scale (VSMS)	Malin's Intelligence Scale for Indian Children (MISIC)
Developmental age (DA)- 6 years 1 month	Social age (SA)- 6 years 3 months	Mental age-5 years 4 months
Developmental quotient (DQ)- 79	Social quotient (SQ)- 81	Intelligence quotient (IQ)-68

Master SS was diagnosed with mild mental retardation, seizure disorder, and behaviour problems.

BEHAVIOURAL ASSESSMENT TOOLS USED

Problem behaviours identifies using Behavioural Assessment Scales for Indian Children (BASIC-MR), Part-B:
1. Pushing others and bangs objects.
2. Slams doors, and tears magazines and books.
3. Tears/pulls threads and screams.
4. Stamps feet and interrupts in-between.
5. Peels skin/wounds and rocks the body.
6. Nods head and talks to self.
7. Hoards unwanted things.
8. Doesn't sit at one place.
9. Pushes others and bangs objects.
10. Lies and steals.

Hierarchy of problem behaviours:
1. Steals money
2. Tells lies and asks for money for every activity.
3. Doesn't sit at one place.
4. Talks to self and rocks the body.

5. Nods head and peels skin/wound.
6. Interrupts while talking.
7. Hoards unwanted objects (stone).
8. Pushes others and bangs objects.
9. Slams doors and tears papers.
10. Screams and stamps feet.

Target Behaviour (TB) identified:

When explained about this step of behaviour modification then mother wanted to deal with his habit of asking for money for everything, crying for money and stealing habit on priority. Her reason to opt for decrease in these behaviours was, a) they don't have much money and b) this habit of crying for money is embarrassing for the family.

1. Asking and crying for money.
2. Stealing money.

Rewards identified:

1. Verbal appreciation
2. Activity

Assets of the child:

1. SS is independent in self-help skills.
2. He can communicate using full sentences.
3. He plays cooperatively with other children.
4. Keeps the money safe in his pocket.
5. With money, stolen or otherwise, buys things for sisters and mother.

Frequency technique was used for recording and to count the number of times SS asks for money and the number of times he steals money.

Table 1: Functional Analysis of TB 1 – Asks for Money

	Why	When	Where	With Whom	Consequence	Significant Information
1	Asked for ₹100 for snacks and soft drinks	Lunch time on 17th May at 2 o'clock	clinic canteen	Mother and maternal aunt	Spent ₹80, did not take back the change, did not finish chips and soft drink	He insists on buying things and gives to others.
2	SS was sleepy, cranky and crying but wanted money to go off to sleep	17th may at 5 o'clock in the evening	Maternal grandmother's place	With his father	Father gave him ₹5 in irritation	SS must have money in his hand before going off to sleep or else cries in monotonous voice for 1 or 2 hours continuously
3	To buy biscuits	18th May, 2 o'clock in the afternoon	Maternal grandmother's place	With his mother.	Mother said she isn't working so hasn't any money. SS asked her to take money from 'mamu' (maternal uncle) who gave him a packet of biscuits not money	

| 4 | SS wanted money to keep in his pocket. | 18th May, same day, at 4 o'clock | Maternal grandmother's place | With his mother | Mother said she didn't have money so he kept quiet | |
| 5 | SS was feeling sleepy | at 8 o'clock in the evening | Maternal grandmother's place | With his mother | Mother wrote this incident in the notebook and didn't give him money. He didn't cry this time as he knows that mother is writing to show to "Doctor ma'am." | |

Table 2: Functional Analysis of TB 2 – Steals Money

	Why	When	Where	With Whom	Consequence
1	SS wanted to buy something for his sisters	17th May, 3 o'clock when mother was busy shopping	local market	At a shop. He stole a bottle of red color	He was confronted at home and was called liar & thief
2	To buy soft drinks & pens for self, mother and sisters	9 o'clock, 18th May when mother was sleeping	Maternal grandmother's place	With his mother He took ₹ 100 from her purse. On enquiry lied about the money	'Mamu', maternal uncle, scolded & tied him to a chair. He cried for 2 hours & promised not to steal again

Functions identified:
1. Tangible
2. Escape

Behavioural package programme:
Target Behaviour 1 (TB1)
1. Differential Reinforcement activity (DRA)
2. Restructure the environment
3. Skill training
4. Over correction
5. Behaviour modification counselling of mother.

Target Behaviour 2 (TB2)
1. Restructure the environment
2. Re-identify and redefine the awards
3. Extinction/ ignore (for crying)
4. Overcorrection

FOLLOW-UP AND FEEDBACK
1. Mother reported that the problem behavior had decreased and SS was not stealing money any more - 23rd May.
2. Mother came and reported that in a marriage function SS needed to go to toilet urgently and there was no ladies' toilet there so she gave him ₹2 and SS had kept quiet - 28th May.

Mother was counselled and explained that in such a situation she could have asked someone to take SS into the gents' toilet instead of giving him money.

3. Mother came with her own mother and reported that SS was listening to her and was not asking for money. She is happy with him but she wanted to discuss about her marital problems. So it was taken up in counselling sessions separately - 13th July.

PARENT COUNSELLING

Brief History: SS is on medication for fits and diurnal enuresis. Mother had brought him for behaviour modification from outstation. He buys grocery and small items for his mother to whom he is very attached.

Significant stresses: His father is illiterate, and not supportive of him or his mother.

Brief summary:
- Physical examination: Age-appropriate looks and well-groomed with no sensory impairment.
- Educational assessment: Studying in class I in normal school but his performance is poor. Keeps coming out of the class on one pretext or the other.
- Psychological assessment: His I.Q. is 68, cries in monotonous voice for hours for need compliance but understands simple instructions and is cooperatively with other children.

Needs Identified for counselling
1. Communication of diagnosis and results of assessments:
   According to the mother, the I.Q. of 68 was better than expected, need for training and behaviour modification was conveyed, and addresses of some Special schools in their locality were provided.
2. Adjustment needs:
   Mother was at adaptation level where she had reconciled and had come to terms with the condition of her third born. Father is at detachment level with meaninglessness and why to waste time, money and energy on the boy.
3. Adaptation Process:
   The mother has shifted to capital city near her parent's house. Both the elder children have been admitted to regular school and SS in a special school. Elder siblings take care of the younger one and understand the need to be in the big city.

Father encourages and reinforces the problem behaviour (asking for money) otherwise he is not interested in what the children do. Father is insecure of SS's mother who is literate, good looking and earns money (she is tailor by profession).

4. Attitude towards child:

   Family members, except father, have a favourable attitude towards SS.

5. Misconceptions:

   Child's father feels that the child should be left alone, nothing can be done. Mother is hopeful and determined to do something and everything not just for SS but for all the three children.

6. Support available:

   The mother is self-earning, social-emotional support is available from child's maternal grandparents and maternal uncles, from paternal step grandmother and step uncles.

7. Needs for imparting information:

   Initially there was lack of information but then following were imparted: -

   a) Need for involvement of not only parents but all the family members in the training programme.

   b) Need for availing various services like behaviour modification, special education services, and medicines.

   c) Information on availability of services like special schools and supported education were given.

8. Need for training and management:

   Behaviour modification programme was explained to the mother highlighting the need to the guidelines consistently, and mother's counselling was done regarding involving the elder siblings in the process.

9. Need for meeting other parents of children with similar conditions:

   While coming regularly to the clinic, mother felt motivated and more determined.

10. There wasn't any need to facilitate programmes initiated by parents of persons with mental retardation.

11. Need for planning future of persons with mental retardation: With family support SS's mother has shifted to capital city from her native place for sake of husband, for better education for elder children and to avail all the services for SS.

Hierarchy of identified needs for counselling:
1. Involvement of father in the training programme.
2. Making him understand the utility of training and effectiveness of training.
3. Need for special school support for SS.
4. Need for better schooling for elder son and specially for elder daughter.
5. Counselling needs for elder children.

Long Term Goal:
Rehabilitation of SS, 1 or 2 sessions required.

Short Term Goal:
Father's counselling

Session 1
Father's counselling was done wherein both the parents were present along with SS. The process was of conversation and hand written short points were used for recording. The husband had visited different department

Evaluation
Husband was impressed with services being provided to his son and also by his wife's efforts. He promised to take care of his cement allergy in the palms, he being a daily wage labourer.

Session 2
Counselling needs of 2 elder children were addressed on 18th August 2006 when the child's mother along with her own mother was present. Again, the process was of conversation and guidance with bullet points

written. Mother was guided to talk with children but not in front of relatives, listen to their concerns and talk to them about the need of shifting. Various needs of SS and for father's vocational adjustment were addressed. The most important points highlighted were that relation with paternal grandmother and uncles need not be broken as they were the support system for the family.

Mother had once attempted suicide, but there was no need for such drastic steps now. She decided to talk to her children openly like adults.

Session 3
28 August
Mother came alone and reported successful conversation with her children and about somewhat cooperative husband who had picked up a daily wages work. SS is doing well in special school. Elder children are going to normal school. She herself is not shouting at and fighting with husband.

-x-

CASE STUDY 2

Master CP

Sex: Male	**DOB**: 27/11/1992
Age: 13 years 5 months	**Father's name**: Mr. AP
Mother's name: Mrs. HP	**Date of Assessment**: 4/05/2006

History
Master CP had come with his mother and maternal aunt with mother's complaint that he misbehaves and abuses others, breaks things and scholastic backwardness (Studying in class 1 for 5 years). No significant history during natal stages was found, he was not immunized, and no

family history of MI, MR or epilepsy. CP belongs to a family of average social-economic status. It is a non-consanguineous marriage.

Session 1
Assessment Tools used
DST (Development Screening Test)
VSMS (Vineland social maturity Scale)

Intelligence test- Malin's Intelligence Scale for Indian children (MISIC)

DST	VSMS	MISIC
Developmental age (DA)- 9 years 11months	Social age (SA)- 9 years 8 months	Mental age - 6 years 2 months
Developmental Quotient (DQ)- 71	Social Quotient (SQ)- 69	Intelligence Quotient (IQ)-46

Master CP was diagnosed with moderate mental retardation having behaviour problems.

Session 2
Behaviour assessment was done using BASIC-MR, Part B. Following Behaviour Problem were identified with consent of mother & aunt.

Behaviour Problems Identified:
1. Kicks & pushes others.
2. Pinches & spits on others
3. Pulls hair & body parts of others
4. Bangs objects & slams doors.
5. Pokes others
6. Tears magazines & breaks objects
7. Interrupts in-between
8. Pulls objects from others.

9. Doesn't sit at one place.
10. Doesn't pay attention to what is told.
11. Doesn't continue a task.
12. Refuses to obey instructions.
13. Does opposite of what is asked.
14. Peels skin/ wounds.

Hierarchy of problem behaviour

Same as above.

Identified Target Behaviours

1. Pinches others
2. Spits on others.

Rewards identified:
1. Bananas-can survive on them.
2. Mango, ice-cream
3. Sweet items
4. Praise from eldest *mamu* (maternal uncle).

Assets of the child:
1. Listens to and obeys *mamu* (maternal uncle).
2. Gives whole money to mothers.

Baselines Recording: Frequency technique was used for both the target behaviours.

Table 1: Functional Analysis of TB 1: Pinches others

	Why	When	Where	With Whom	Consequence
1	Younger brother hit him back	While watching TV	At home	Younger brother	Ran away & sat on the roof till lunch time
2	Elder sister had slapped him for spitting on her	While cleaning the utensils	At home	Elder sister	Ran away from home when reprimanded by mother saying sister was lying. Came back in evening, had food and slept
3	Younger cousin was playing	While playing	At home	Mamu's daughter	Mami Maternal uncle's wife) slapped him, he shouted but before mother could come, he ran out-side

Table 2: Functional Analysis of TB 2: Spits on others.

	Why	When	Where	With Whom	Consequence
1	Young cousin was sleeping	6:30 am	Aunt's place	Aunt's daughter	Mother came and beat him. He ran away with a grown-up boy to work place, came in the evening and had food and then went to sleep.
2	Elder sister was cleaning the utensils	Noon	At home	Elder sister	Sister slapped him. Later while going out he pinched her

Functions Identified:
1. Attention seeking
2. Tangible
3. Escape

Behaviour Package programme:
1. Restructure the environment
2. Differential Reinforcement Activity
3. Re-schedule of daily activity
4. Over-correction
5. Verbal pleasure/ displeasure especially by mamu (maternal uncle).
6. B.M. counselling of parents.

Significant decrease was reported by mother in follow up sessions. Asked her to continue with the programme.

Parent counselling

Significant stress:
CP will do anything for strangers and outsiders but won't listen to his own family members. Father is busy in his shop.

Brief summary:
- Physical examination: Looks age appropriate, well-built and well groomed.
- Educational assessment: Doesn't study at all, studying in class 1 for 5 years.
- Psychological assessment: With IQ of 46 but developmental quotient and social quotient at 71 and 69 respectively he understands and comprehends simple instructions as well as social situations.

Identifying Needs For counselling

1. Communication of diagnosis and results of assessment: Mother had known and expected the diagnostic result.
2. Adjustment needs: Parents are at adaptation level, with reconciliation and coming to terms with the child's condition.
3. Family environment: CP fights, pinches and spits over his siblings and cousins with no regard to age or situation. Mother is overprotective of him and parental relation is cordial.
4. Attitude: towards CP is favorable
5. Misconception: is that he runs away and sits at the shops owned by close friends and relatives so it is ok. He should listen to mother. Family has social, emotional and financial support. All relatives live in the same street and near-by.
6. Need for imparting information: Need for parental as well as family involvement for strict and persist implementation of B.M programming was imparted to mother.
7. Training and management: B.M. counselling and B.M. programme with explanation was imparted.
8. The need to meet other parents with similar conditions wasn't expressed.
9. The need to facilitate programmes initiated by parents and persons with Mental Retardation wasn't expressed nor felt by the counsellor.
10. Need for training in skills and decrease in Behaviour problem with help of BMP was given importance by mother as well as the aunt.

Hierarchy of needs:

1. Activity scheduling of the child.
2. Keeping a track of his social environment (peer group).
3. Skill training

Session 1

Mother was counselled to understand the need to follow Behaviour Management Programme (BMP). Mother and maternal aunt had to come for the sessions. The process was of conversation and technique used was writing bullet points. Mother decided to be strict with BMP and its application and implementation.

Session 2

Mother reported significant decrease in problem behaviours and compliance by the child in follow-up sessions.

9

REHABILITATION

Rehabilitation is the process of helping an individual achieve the highest level of function, independence, and quality of life possible. People with disabilities, whether congenital or acquired, may face personal, social and situational barriers not allowing them to effectively function in the society. Some barriers are inherent in the disabling condition, while others arise out of myths prevalent in the society and this contribute towards a devaluation or neglect of persons who are different. The word "rehabilitation" has originated from Medieval Latin. It literally means restoration to good health.

Rehabilitation implies restoration/maintenance of/improvement in physical, mental and emotional states of a person of any age suffering from any disability. Social needs of the individual, his/her family and the society are crucial factors in the rehabilitation process.

The process of rehabilitation is concerned with preventing further deterioration of the condition and with alleviating the effects of appropriate treatment. The rehabilitation programme must be developed in response to the uniqueness of each person- his/her history, ability, disability, environment and expectations.

The root word for rehabilitation is "Habilitation" that means the process through which persons born with certain impairment are helped to channelize their residual capacities to their maximum development so that he/she would live as normal a life as possible. To better understand the concept, let us take the example of the word 'habitat' i.e., the natural environment in which an organism is born and survives naturally having the right skills. The problem arises when either something goes wrong with the environment forcing the organism to adapt for survival or die, or something goes wrong with the organism forcing it to re-learn and adapt for survival or perish.

The difference between the two terms are as follows:

S. No	Rehabilitation	Habilitation
1.	To help a person with lost functions	To help a person born with disability
2.	Restoration of abilities	Development of abilities that never existed or were delayed
3.	Development of long or/ and short-term programmes depending upon the needs of an individual	It is a long-term programme
4.	Need to develop fundamental capabilities, knowledge, experience & attitudes	Need to develop basic skills of day-today life through structured skill training programmes
5.	Deals with enhancement of one's own environment	Deals with the treatment & training of persons with mental retardation, autism, & sensory impairment etc.
6.	Broad concept includes habilitation for all round development	It is a specific concept

WHO defines rehabilitation as the combined and coordinated use of medical, social, educational, and vocational measures for training or re-training the disabled individual to the highest possible level of functional ability and enabling the disabled individual to achieve social integration.

SOME DEFINITIONS OF REHABILITATION

➤ "Rehabilitation is a problem solving and educational process aimed at reducing the disability and handicap experienced by someone as a result of a disease, always within the limitations imposed both by available resources and by underlying disease." – ICDH. It is acting upon pathology, or disability, or upon the intervening variables in order to reduce the handicap. In essence, it is the management of change.

➤ "Rehabilitation is the study and application of bio-psycho-social principles to persons who have physical, sensory, cognitive, developmental or emotional disabilities."

➤ "Rehabilitation is a process of active change by which a person who has become disabled acquires the knowledge and skills needed for optimal physical, psychological social function."

➤ "Rehabilitation is the application of all measures aimed at reducing the impact of disabling and handicapping conditions, and enabling the disabled and handicapped people to achieve social integration." – D Lindsay McLellan

➤ "Rehabilitation is a set of influences, procedures and resources to be applied both to the disabled person and to the environment".

➤ "Rehabilitation involves the prevention of disability and the maintenance of social role and not simply recovery of or improvement in function."

➤ "Rehabilitation is the process of restoring a person's ability to live and work as normally as possible after a disabling injury or illness".

NEED FOR REHABILITATION

Rehabilitation is a highly person-centered health strategy examples of which include:

• Exercises to regain the ability to swallow or upper-limb retraining to regain coordination, dexterity and movement of an affected limb following a stroke.

- Interventions that improve safety and independence at home and reduce the risk of falls for an older person, such as balance training or modifying their home environment.
- Early interventions to address developmental outcomes of a child with cerebral palsy, such as fitting an orthosis, or providing training in sensory integration and self-care, which in turn can improve participation in education, play, and family and community activities.
- Interventions that optimize surgical outcomes after a hip fracture, including exercise prescription, provision of a walking aid and education about hip movements to avoid during the recovery process.
- Cognitive behavioural therapy and interventions aiming to increase exercise for an individual with depression.
- Interventions that support daily activities and community access for individuals with vision loss, such as providing strategies to complete personal care tasks and training in the use of a white cane.
- Convalescence and some period of re-adjustment for anyone whose normal functioning has been disrupted by illness or injury.
- An active programme of rehabilitation can make the difference between semi-dependent life at home and a totally dependent existence in an institution for a young man who has damaged brain and physical disability due to an accident.
- The housewife severely burnt by boiling water may need to be rehabilitated if she has to pick the threads of housework again.
- The old woman who falls and breaks her hip bone needs more than the provision of a walking frame.
- The middle-aged woman with progressive breast cancer needs more than a prosthesis to compensate for her lost breast.

Is there any person who is or has been a patient, who would not benefit from rehabilitation? This ideal state may not be easily attained, and any rehabilitation programme brings with it certain moral and ethical considerations. In fact, rehabilitation is a continuous process.

HISTORY OF REHABILITATION

(The source of this material is not known to the author as it was copied when she was a student studying in MPhil making notes for herself)

Rehabilitation, as we know and understand today, started in the late 1940's due to the ravaging effects of the two world wars. In fact, vast amount of information about disability has been made available in scientific and logical manner since then. But the model of rehabilitation was largely one of vocational output. It was out of necessity and experience, that new ideas developed.

Then it came to the notice of the professionals that individuals with disabilities failed in outside world and they run into problems associated with different aspects of their lifestyles. The cause wasn't in the vocational area or in the individual's inability to do his or her job but rather in the inability to deal with various aspects of social, family, personal and emotional life i.e., due to lack of surviving skills.

Thus, came the understanding that it is necessary to collaborate across the sciences and that through trans-disciplinary involvement rehabilitation process can successfully be accomplished.

PHASE I:
The people with disabilities were either drowned or exposed to the elements to die with the slogan "Survival of the fittest", and "No right to live".

PHASE II: 1600's onwards
A social change came about which was part of the French Revolution where food, clothes, shelter etc. were provided to the people with disabilities.

PHASE III: 1775-1885

a) It was acknowledged that some people have special needs.

b) Separate schools and residential institutions were created for them.

c) Generally religious and/or charitable organizations used to look after the disabled.

d) They were removed from the family and the community.

e) At first programmes were developed in vocational trainings and later in education.

f) Blindness was the first disability that was addressed from education point of view and the first school for the blind was opened in Paris in 1785.

PHASE IV: 1885-1945

a) It was recognised that the society has responsibility towards its disabled population.

b) Social awareness led to the creation of more specialized services within the segregated special systems.

c) Many more schools were started.

d) Words like subnormal and handicapped were being used now.

PHASE V: 1945-1970

a) This period saw a rapid expansion of services and improvement in the quality of rehabilitation services especially in war-related areas.

b) Human Resource Development in rehabilitation services and more specialized fields opened up.

c) Specific legislation for the disabled were developed.

d) The concept of "segregation" from the family and community still continued.

e) Experiments in early intervention started. It was the phase where legal rights of people with disabilities was focussed upon.

PHASE VI: 1970-1990

a) Individualization, normalization, integration and mainstreaming of the people with disabilities began.

b) Importance of early intervention confirmed by empirical evidence and age of admission into special schools were lowered.

c) Early childhood education, child development and special education – converged to become Early Childhood Special Education (ECSE) – special education is a system of services and support for children with disabilities.

d) Integrated education began – at first partial and later total.

e) WHO and UN bodies took special interests in Community Based Rehabilitation (CBR).

f) Organizations of disabled people grew in number.

g) Rights issues as opposed to welfare and charity issues took precedence.

h) Alma Mata Declaration for health for all, and primary health care concepts came to be practised.

i) International Year of the Disabled UN (1981) Convention on rights of the Child (especially articles 2 & 23).

j) UN resolution – from segregation to integration to inclusion.

PHASE VII: 1990 onwards

a) UN Decade of the Disabled Persons.

b) Education for All (EFA) Forum (Framework for Action to Meet Basic Learning Needs). Para 8 "expansion of early intervention especially for the poor, disabled and for disabled children". UNESCO deals with these issues.

c) ESCAP Decade of the Disabled for Asia Pacific Region.

d) UN standard rules on Equalization for opportunities for Persons with Disabilities (PWD).

e) International Labour Office (ILO) Position paper on equitable training.

f) UNESCO Salamanca Statement and Framework for Action on Special Needs Education issued after International Conference in Spain June 1994.

The success of the inclusive school depends considerably on early identification, assessment and stimulation of the very young child with special educational needs. Early Childhood care and education programmes for children up to 6 years of age ought to be developed and/ or re-oriented to promote physical, intellectual and social development as well as school readiness. These programmes have major economic value for the individual, family, and society in preventing aggravations of the disabling conditions. Disability issues are now considered to be part of Human Rights issues.

The concept of rehabilitation started from extermination and shifted to segregation then to integration and now it is related to inclusion. In fact, there has been a conceptual shift from integration to inclusion. To understand the concept, let us take the example of dal (lentils) grains and the grains of uncooked rice. Mixing of rice grains and dal is Integration where the grains can be separated when needed. But the mixing of milk and water is Inclusion where the two cannot be separated easily.

IMPORTANCE OF REHABILITATION SERVICES

A report by WHO:

Longevity of life has added to an increasing population of older people and as a result of this ageing population, there is an increasing number of persons with disabilities. Better medical services and better prenatal care has increased the chances for children with disabilities to survive. These children are outliving their parents and care givers. Rampant non-communicable diseases have led to an increase in the number of persons with chronic disease and disabilities. Injuries are rising because of increase in violence, conflict and traffic accidents. As a result of all this, the demand for rehabilitation services has increased.

It is being acknowledged that the disabling effects of disease, accidental injuries and congenital defects comprise one of the greatest responsibilities for not only medicine but the society itself. Rehabilitation services have extended to every type of disability, mental as well as physical. It focuses on vocational training and adequate functioning in all areas of life. Restoration of accidental injuries, emotional breakdown, acute diseases, to develop the capabilities of individuals affected by mental retardedness, learning disabilities, congenital defects, even the disabilities due to old age (that can be delayed but not avoided)- are all included in rehabilitation.

The term 'disabled' has been replaced by 'especially abled'. This field of rehabilitation is an upcoming and new field, and as the day passes, new areas are being included in it. Rehabilitation involves training of the patient in such a way that he/she may attain his/her maximum potential for a normal living, be it physically, psychologically, socially or vocationally.

It is also manpower intensive depending a great deal on the quality and number experts deployed in this task. These services grew out of parental and relatives' concern for the handicapped child, and out of compassion that and charitable dispensation of religious and charitable institutions. It's a multidimensional activity that involves various kinds of disabilities and each disability has aspects like restorative, educational, vocational, social integration etc.

Rehabilitation shortens the hospital stay, decreases the re-admission rate, results in earlier return to employment, and it reduces the need for costly maintenances services. For the success of rehabilitation programme, the recipient person must be an active partner and not just a passive recipient.

OBJECTIVES OF REHABILITATION

    a. To develop services for meeting medical, psychological and social needs of persons with disabilities.

    b. To improve social-emotional relationships between the handicapped and the non-handicapped in order to make these relations more compatible and more enriching.

c. To enlarge free movement in the physical and social environment of the disabled and disabled and deprived, and the creation of greater opportunities for the satisfaction of needs.

PURPOSE OF REHABILITATION
a. Reducing the disability.
b. Acquiring new strategies and skills through which the impact of the disability could be minimised.
c. Making changes in the environment like, changing the behaviour and attitude of non-disabled people, so that the impairment and disability no longer confer a handicap.

MODELS OF REHABILITATION

The model of rehabilitation involves a number of primary features. First there is a recognition that mental handicap, mental illness and physical disability are the result of a variety of interacting primary and secondary negative impacts along with primary and secondary positive impacts. In order to understand the rehabilitation process and to apply an effective model of rehabilitation to each individual, these positive and negative impacts must be recognized and detailed at the programme building stage for each individual. They represent, in one sense, the quality which recognizes that each individual is unique, and determined for that individual a specialized and independent programme.

There are six models of rehabilitation:
   I. Biomedical Model
   II. Social Model
   III. Psychological Model
   IV. Vocational Model
   V. Educational Model
   VI. Community Based Rehabilitation Model

I. BIOMEDICAL MODEL OF REHABILITATION

Prescription of medicine, corrective surgery, application of special treatments such as hydrotherapy and range-of-motion exercises, adapted sports, use of such equipment as respirators or kidney machines, orthotic and prosthetic devices, and functional aids.

Medical rehabilitation has its origins in the treatment given to soldiers in the I World War. Since then, both medicine and rehabilitation have developed but medical advances have greatly outstripped those of rehab.

Basic Health Measures
Improvement of health by way of sanitation and hygiene, provision of adequate nutrition, immunization programmes and public health education can reduce and prevent disabilities.

Desirable Health Measures
It is important to promote positive health and improve health practices in pregnancy and child rearing, particularly to high-risk mothers and children. Genetic counselling, family planning and health education in schools will aid in prevention of disability.

Disability Prevention
Prenatal diagnosis, neo-natal screening, health surveillance, and medical and surgical treatment of associated impairments and diseases is very important.

Early Intervention
Early identification and early intervention can foster optimum growth and development of children with disabilities. By availability of services at the earliest possible stage, severe invalidity can be prevented as a consequence of which the disabled are enabled to return speedily to normal living.

II. SOCIAL MODEL OF REHABILITATION

It is carried out through participation in discussion groups, socio-therapy, sex and marital education, self-government and self-advocacy activities, day and resident camps, and a wide range clubs and recreational activities. It is concerned with ameliorating welfare problems primarily the financial, housing and transport problems experienced by Persons With Disabilities (PWD).

Social Developmental Approach It aims at developing positive societal attitudes and awareness about the problems of disability to provide effective services for the disabled.

Social Services Approach aims directly at providing social and rehabilitative services for the disabled. Institutional and continuous care and treatment may be required for the severely disabled individuals.

With increase in vocational programmes the number of Persons With Disabilities (PWD) in employment also increased but with it increased the work failure. Some of the reason quoted, truthfully, for the same are as follows:

- Lack of vocational skills for a particular job
- Inappropriate job placement
- Lack of social skills

Thus, it was recognised that social educational skills are very important in the preparation of handicapped young adults for vocational placements.

Social educational, social living skills, aids of daily living (AOL), or life skills need to be recognized and taught.

The social educational continuum is also conceived as starting from basic concrete skills, such as word recognition, through expansion of language, to more formal educational skills in reading and writing, beginning with practical abilities such as signing one's name. the application of these skills in a variety of community areas is also viewed as part of the continuum. Such a continuum must involve self-assertive training, including the growth of social maturity to confront and effectively deal with challenging situations in the environment.

This leads naturally into the area of sexuality training.

Handicapped individuals often suffer with poor self-image which can be boosted by, first, providing a number of basic and useful community skills as well as communication skills.

The social educational continuum covers a wide range of skills such as budgeting, time management, transportation and social sight reading, to name a few. Increased understanding of social educational need was such that by the beginning of 1970's many programmes had developed basic social educational training.

III. PSYCHOLOGICAL MODEL OF REHABILITATION

It consists of personal counselling, psychotherapy wherever needed, supportive and motivational measures directed toward increased self-acceptance and full cooperation in the entire rehabilitation efforts.

It includes activities designed to meet special needs such as instructions for the blind, lip reading, sign language for the deaf, educational therapy to the learning disabled, service for the home-bound, intensive treatment and readjustment training for the mentally ill.

Developmental psychology has provided overall view of the sequence of the behavioural development that has practical relevance to the child or the adult who, due to accident, stress or other damage, has regressed to an earlier level of performance. It has become acceptable to apply knowledge about child development in the design and application of the programmes in rehabilitation field. When the practitioner understands and systematically applies such knowledge to the delivery of individualized and structured intervention, more effective changes in performance can occur. The process of rehabilitation involves the enhancement of those structures which accelerate normal development.

IV. VOCATIONAL MODEL OF REHABILITATION

Vocational rehabilitation may be defined as the process of inducting or re-inducting the people with disabilities into the workforce. It is a term which shouldn't be seen as synonym for occupational rehabilitation.

The present employment scenario and the competent as well as demanding nature of many jobs severely restrict the chances of PWD securing employment. Hence, it becomes imperative that young adults with disabilities should receive careful training and preparation to help them not only find but also keep a job.

Vocational rehabilitation involves vocational training for placement in non-sheltered as well as sheltered workplaces, vocational training for self-employment and assistant for placement in suitable jobs in the labour market.

Though, paid work is a vital force in life of an adult, Cushan (1984) suggests that work should be considered in two inter-related dimensions viz.

a. Economic i.e., financial support
b. Social i.e., a source of self-esteem, social contacts, self-discipline and satisfaction.

OBJECTIVES
(*This material is taken from 'Foundations of Physical Rehabilitation – A Management Approach'. Doreen Bauer*)

1. To provide appropriate vocational counselling based on:
   - An assessment of the client's abilities, disabilities and coping skills
   - An appreciation of the client's goals and wishes
   - A thorough knowledge of the possible employment options

2. To assist the client in seeking and obtaining employment, acting as an advocate/adviser as required.

3. To design necessary educational or training programmes so as to equip the client with skills which have potential.

4. To educate and counsel employees and unions seeking understanding and cooperation especially in terms of:
   - Environmental modifications if required
   - Work station design
   - Progressive entry into the role, either in relation to time or workload
   - Possible strategies such as part – time hours or job sharing

5. To make appropriate use of any legislative or financial support which may apply:
   - Anti-discrimination legislation
   - Legislation in relation to compensation (e.g., industrial injuries, motor vehicle injuries)
   - Government programmes which may finance equipment/ environmental modifications

6. To provide continuous support until the goals of vocational rehabilitation have been achieved.

7. To assist the client, develop alternative goals should employment prove beyond attainment.

V.   EDUCATIONAL MODEL OF REHABILITATION

It entails education of the disabled children as well as adults both formal and non-formal. The education of children with disabilities has increasingly become the responsibility of the educational authorities. Children with special needs can benefit from education involving specific methods needed to teach these children.

In focusing on the strategy of compulsory education to all (SSA), the development of special education services needs to be enhanced. Education is the only medium of inclusion and maintenance of PWD.

Education should lead to independence, special education to special children, self-advocacy to PWD, and help organise as well as run self-help groups.

VI. COMMUNITY BASED REHABILITATION

Community Based Rehabilitation (CBR) is a strategy aimed at enhancement of the quality of life of the people with disability by improving service delivery, by providing more equitable opportunities, and by promoting and protecting their human rights.

CBR is to rehabilitate the disabled persons to achieve total development through the combined efforts of the individual, the family, the community and various social service organizations. The main aim is to help the persons with disability to gain equal rights as that of normal persons and make them an integral part of the society. It deals with all aspects of development, prevention of disability, early identification and early intervention, rehabilitation of the disabled, empowerment of the disabled as well as community development.

OBJECTIVES
1. Creation of awareness in the community
2. Changing the attitude of the family members and the community
3. Establishment of a comprehensive model
4. Promote voluntary effort to establish rehabilitation centres
5. Promote simple, appropriate and cost-effective technologies
6. Create a cadre of multi-disciplinary workers and professionals

ASSESSMENT IN REHABILITATION

It is apparent that intelligence is a poor predictor of overall life skills performance. Intelligence measures appear to be correlated with educational attainment when predicting specific educational skills, but not necessarily associated with social skills attainment. If one develops a socially oriented curriculum, then intelligence does not seem to be a relevant predictor of success.

It therefore becomes important to recognize what the educational or rehabilitation goals are, and what expectations are contained within any particular curriculum.

Another important concept is that social skills might be far more important in terms of whether an individual can/can't survive in society. Psychologists and other professionals need intelligence test data within the rehabilitation process to provide them with some type of marker which supports other findings. It also is used as baseline to interpret certain specific difficulties.

Functional Assessment and curriculum development also have great impact on programme delivery and planning as they determine the needs and strengths of PWD.

FUNCTIONS OF ASSESSMENT

1. To describe an individual at a particular point in time, in terms of intellectual, social, emotional, educational, and allied variables, with reference to a normative or contrast population.
2. To predict performance of an individual at a future point in time.
3. To provide a profile of assets and deficits in order to determine a starting point for further intervention or training.
4. To provide an objective means of monitoring progress of an individual or a group of individuals over time.
5. Authorities need to use behavioural assessment techniques for the purpose of classification and categorization and this in turn is helpful for government benefits, scholarships and reservation in jobs. The predictive ability of the tests within the field of disability is very poor and it underestimates the actual success on different tasks. Test results should not be used for long term prediction, and when used for short term prediction they should

be employed for specific prescriptive purposes. Assessment is a continuous process and multi-dimensional in nature.

In rehabilitation, before a given treatment plan could be developed, it might be necessary to determine such factors as age, education, transferability of skills, mental ability, prior work experience, and related phenomenon.

CONSTRAINTS AND CONFLICTS

1. Opportunities for rehabilitation are unevenly distributed throughout the country and in some areas, they are entirely lacking. There is a big gap between the number of professionals available and those required.
2. Major constraint is of finance which for health care is limited. When the funding agencies stop the fund, after completion of a major project, the rehabilitation programme suffers.
3. Some professionals plan rehabilitation programme based on clinical experience and not in consultation with the patient or his family. They give the impression that they know what the best is for the patient.
4. The shift of population towards urban places, progress toward poverty in rural areas, decline in extended families to look after the needs of their disabled members thereby making the disabled people a burden on their families.
5. The burden of caring for a disabled person and the stigma attached to the disability can sometimes make the community refuse cooperation in any rehabilitation programme.
6. The attack on disability is in its initial stages.
7. Development in research effort is seriously hampered due to insufficient funds.
8. Many obvious needs of the disabled are not being met, such as access to public transport, barrier free residences and schools, and opportunities to avail the advanced functional aids.

9. Chronic disorders and disabilities of every type are generally prevalent among low-income families and the problem of poverty is wide spread.

10. Attitude of society, relatives and the patient him/herself act as hindrance.

   a. Pressure groups can often act against the best interests of people requiring care. The campaigners are probably quite caring people, but their fears of plummeting house prices and noisy or embarrassing incidents are, to them, real. How can one reassure the mother of tiny infant who comes out of a shop and discovers a mentally handicapped man peering into the pram and making strange noises? The mother doesn't know that he is harmless and loves babies though he looks odd and behaves strangely. This mother joins the pressure group which fights against having a house in her street taken over for 6 mentally handicapped people.

   b. Attitude of Relatives: let's take an example of eight-year-old girl suffering from Cerebral Palsy who was cared for in a special residential school. By the term end, the physiotherapist had succeeded in getting her to walk. But when she returned, she was back in her wheelchair. On enquiry, she said that for her mother it is easier if she is in the chair. The whole process started again. But again after returning from holidays, she was in wheelchair because her mother wanted her to be there. Both gained something from what was happening. The mother here needed counselling.

   c. Sometimes the patient him/herself is the constraint in the process of rehabilitation. Being at home may be more congenial than being at work. The relationship which the patient has established between the therapist and his fellow rehabilitees may be more satisfying than any others he knows. Some people thrive on other people. Well-meaning friends can play havoc with the patient's recovery be well-intentioned but misplaced advice.

Dr Neerja Pandey

Four E's are the guiding principle for rehabilitation that is: **Enlightenment, Education Employment,** and **E**mpowerment. Empowerment of women and girl child takes the central place in the whole of rehabilitation concept as women are basic caregivers to family members. But in the case of a women with disability – her needs are not met with and she becomes the most neglected one.

Rehabilitation Council of India, the statutory body under the Ministry of Social Justice and Empowerment, has been trying to undertake programmes of continuing rehabilitation education so that the country has a reservoir of trained people who could impart the best possible training to children and adults with disabilities.

The objective of the programme is to ensure that the knowledge of rehabilitation professionals is updated from time to time so as to provide the best possible services to the people with disabilities.

When we talk of helping the PWD, it doesn't mean somebody outside our vicinity. We ourselves are not above disability. So, we have to put ourselves forward, in other person's shoes and think of helping ourselves. If and when all the professionals start thinking in this manner only then the field of rehabilitation will get a proper and desired push in the right direction.

PARENTAL ROLE

Parents live with the child throughout his/her life and continuous parental influence tends to be the greatest force in the child's life. It, thus, becomes the most important task for the experts to help the parents in acquiring the knowledge and skills to deal effectively with the child. It is very simplistic to assume that the family would take on the responsibility for the care of the disabled.

The family members need counselling and training so that they are able to cope with the uphill task of bearing the emotional, psychological and financial expenses. Sensitivity to the emotional needs of the parents at the time of initial diagnosis is needed the most. Rehabilitation professionals have to train themselves keeping these aspects in mind.

Employment of Persons with Disabilities (PWD) is the toughest task of rehabilitation. For this aspect following are needed to be done:

a. Job oriented training and career counselling facilities
b. Preparation of PWD for suitable employment
c. Convincing the employers to extend employment
d. Counselling of family members and the community
e. Ensure effective implementation of legislative measures
f. Involve government machinery actively in the process

- Rehabilitation shortens the hospital stay and decreases the re-admission into the hospital. It increases the rate of return to employment and reduces the need for costly maintenance services.

Dr Neerja Pandey

10
REFERENCES

- About Fragile X Syndrome. National Human Genome Research Institute (NIH). https://www.genome.gov/Genetic-Disorders/Fragile-X-Syndrome#:~:text=This%20condition%20is%20inherited%20in,sufficient%20to%20cause%20the%20condition.

- Batshaw, M. L., Roizen, N. J., Lotrecchiano, G. R. (2013). Children with Disabilities. 7th Edition, Paul H. Brooks Publishing Co., www.brookspublishing.com, ISBN 978-1-59857-194-3.

- Bauer, Doreen. (1989). *Foundations of Physical Rehabilitation – A Management Approach.* ISBN-13:9780443037160, Churchill Livingstone (publisher).

- Bijou, Sidney W., Redd, William H. (2015). Behaviour Therapy for Children. *American Handbook of Psychiatry*, Vol 5. International Psychotherapy Institute. https://www.freepsychotherapybooks.org/ebook/behavior-modification/

- Binder, Carl V. (2016). Behaviour Modification. International Psychotherapy Institute, from '*The Psychotherapy Guidebook*'.https://www.freepsychotherapybooks.org/ebook/behavior-modification/

- Carr, E. G., Dunlap, G., Horner, R.H., Koegel, R. L., Turnbull, A. P., Sailor, W., Anderson, J., Albin, R. W., Koegel, L. K., Fox, L. (2002). Positive Behaviour Support. *Journal of Positive Behavior Intervention*,https://www.researchgate.net/publication/43155726. DOI:10.1177/109830070200400102

- Chromosome Abnormalities Fact Sheet. National Human Genome Research Institute (NIH). https://www.genome.gov/about-genomics/fact-sheets/Chromosome-Abnormalities-Fact-Sheet

- Duchenne Muscular Dystrophy (DMD). Muscular Dystrophy Association. https://www.mda.org/disease/duchenne-muscular-dystrophy#:~:text=Duchenne%20muscular%20dystrophy%20(DMD)%20is,four%20conditions%20known%20as%20dystrophinopathies.

- Female Reproductive System. Cleveland Clinic. https://my.clevelandclinic.org/health/articles/9118-female-reproductive-system

- Gender and Genetics. Genomic Resource Centre. World Health Organization. https://www.who.int/genomics/gender/en/index1.html

- Goldfinger, Karen Pomerantz, Andrew, M. (2014). Psychological Assessment and Report Writing. Second edition. Sage Publication. Pp 12-27.

- Hemophilia. MedlinePlus. https://medlineplus.gov/genetics/condition/hemophilia/#:~:text=Hemophilia%20A%20and%20hemophilia%20B,sufficient%20to%20cause%20the%20condition.

- How Many Eggs are Woman Born with? Healthline. https://www.healthline.com/health/womens-health/how-many-eggs-does-a-woman-have

- Lalonde F. Prevention of Disabilities. A summary of Graduate Student Project. SSTA Research Centre Report # 94-07a. https://saskschoolboards.ca/wp-content/uploads/94-07a.htm

- Madhavan, T., Kalyan, M., Naidu, S., Peshawaria, R., Narayan, J. (1989). *Mental Retardation – A Manual for Psychologists*. Sree Ramana Process Pvt. Ltd., National Institute for the Mentally Handicapped,

Secunderabad, 500009. Sri Ramana Process, Secunderabad. https://niepid.nic.in/public.php.

- Madhavan, T., Kalyan, M., Naidu, S., Peshawaria, R., Narayan, J. (1989). *Mental Retardation – A Manual for Psychologists.* National Institute for the Mentally Handicapped, Secunderabad, 500009. Sri Ramana Process, Secunderabad. https://niepid.nic.in/public.php.

- McLeod, S. A. (2019). *Case Study Method.* Simply Psychology. https://www.simplypsychology.org/case-study.html

- Nina N. Powell-Hamilton (2020). Overview of Sex Chromosome Anomalies. https://www.msdmanuals.com/professional/pediatrics/chromosome-and-gene-anomalies/overview-of-sex-chromosome-anomalies

- Persha, A. J., Kumar, T. C. S., Narayan, J., Kari, M. L. (2003). Reaching and Programming for Identification of Disabilities (RAPID). A package on Prevention and Early Detection of Childhood Disabilities for Grass Root Level Workers. Sree Ramana Process Pvt. Ltd., ISBN 81 86594 98 1., National Institute for the Mentally Handicapped, Secunderabad. https://niepid.nic.in/public.php

- Peshawaria, R., Venkatesan, S. (1992). Behavioral Approach in Teaching Mentally Retarded Children – A Manual for Teachers. Sree Ramana Process Pvt. Ltd., National Institute for the Mentally Handicapped, Secunderabad, 500009. https://niepid.nic.in/public.php

- Peshawaria, R., Venkatesan, S. (1992). Behavioral Approach in Teaching Mentally Retarded Children – A Manual for Teachers. National Institute for the Mentally Handicapped, Secunderabad, 500009. https://niepid.nic.in/public.php

- Rehabilitation 2030 Initiative. World Health Organization. https://www.who.int/initiatives/rehabilitation-2030

- Rehabilitation Council of India. http://www.rehabcouncil.nic.in/

- Report Writing. Deakin University.

  https://www.deakin.edu.au/students/studying/study-support/academic-skills/report-writing#2different

- Rights of Persons with Disabilities Act, 2016. Department of Empowerment of Persons with Disabilities (Divyangjan), Ministry of Social Justice and Empowerment, Government of India. http://disabilityaffairs.gov.in/content/page/acts.php

- Shorter Women have Shorter Pregnancies. Science Daily. https://www.sciencedaily.com/releases/2015/08/150818153507.htm

- Sickle Cell Anemia. National Center for Advancing Translational Sciences (NIH). Genetic and Rare Diseases Information Center (GARD). https://rarediseases.info.nih.gov/diseases/8614/sickle-cell-anemia#:~:text=Sickle%20cell%20anemia%20is%20inherited,and%20symptoms%20of%20the%20condition.

- Single Gene Disorders. Understanding Genetics: A District of Columbia Guide for Parents and Health Professional. 2010. Genetic Alliance, District of Columbia, Department of Health. https://www.ncbi.nlm.nih.gov/books/NBK132154/#:~:text=Some%20of%20the%20more%20common,degrees%20of%20severity%20and%20phenotype.

- The National Trust. Department of Empowerment of Persons with Disabilities (Divyangjan), Ministry of Social Justice and Empowerment, Government of India. https://www.thenationaltrust.gov.in/content/innerpage/introduction.php

- Unique Disability ID. Department of Empowerment of Persons with Disabilities, Ministry of Social Justice and Empowerment, Government of India. https://www.india.gov.in/spotlight/unique-disability-id

- Whitman, Myron A. (1975). Behaviour Modification: Introduction and Implications. *DePaul University, University Libraries,* Volume 24, Issue 4, Summer 1975. https://core.ac.uk/download/pdf/232968194.pdf